DEVON'S PAST
AN AERIAL VIEW

Frances Griffith

DEVON BOOKS

First published in Great Britain in 1988 by Devon Books

ISBN: 0 86114–833–9

British Library Cataloguing-in-Publication Data
Griffith, Frances
Devon's past : an aerial view.
1. Devon. Antiquities. Sites. Sources of evidence. Aerial photographs
I. Title
936.2′35

Printed and bound in Great Britain by A. Wheaton & Co. Ltd

Produced by the Amenities and Countryside Officer, Peter Hunt, for the Amenities and Countryside Committee through the Property Department Director, Andrew Smy.

DEVON BOOKS

Official Publisher to Devon County Council

An imprint of Wheaton Publishers Ltd, a member of Maxwell/Pergamon Publishing Corporation plc

Wheaton Publishers Ltd, Hennock Road, Marsh Barton, Exeter, Devon EX2 8RP Tel: 0392 74121; Telex 42794 (WHEATN G)

SALES

Direct sales enquiries to Devon Books at the address above.

Trade sales to: Town & Country Books, P.O. Box 31, Newton Abbot, Devon TQ12 5XH.
Tel: 08047 2541

Contents

Introduction 7

Select Bibliography 13

Acknowledgements 15

Plate 1 Start Point 17

Plate 2 Cliffs at Hartland Point, North-west Devon 18

Plate 3 Higher Kiln Quarry, Buckfastleigh 19

Plate 4 Chudleigh Caves 20

Plate 5 Baggy Point, Georgeham 21

Plate 6 Westward Ho! 22

Plate 7 Beer Head 23

Plate 8 Hembury Hillfort, Payhembury 24

Plate 9 Henge between Bow and North Tawton 25

Plates 10, 11 Ceremonial Monuments on Dartmoor 26

Plate 12 Five Barrows, Exmoor 28

Plate 13 Crownhill Down, South-west Dartmoor 29

Plates 14–16 Ring Ditches 30

Plate 17 Reaves, Rippon Tor, Dartmoor 32

Plate 18 Reaves, Easdon Down, Dartmoor 34

Plate 19 Prehistoric Enclosures, Walkhampton 35

Plate 20 Riders Rings, South Brent, Dartmoor 36

Plate 21 Grimspound, Manaton, Dartmoor 37

Plate 22 Throwleigh Common, Dartmoor 38

Plate 23 Settlement Enclosure at Shaugh Moor, South Dartmoor 39

Plate 24 Shoulsbarrow Hillfort, Exmoor 40

Plates 25, 26 Milber Down Hillfort, near Newton Abbot 41

Plate 27 Hillfort, Stoke Rivers 42

Plate 28 Enclosure near Bideford 43

Plate 29 Embury Beacon, Hartland 44

Plate 30 Field System, East Ogwell 45

Plates 31, 32 Settlement site at Pond Farm, Alphington 46

Plate 33 Central Exeter in 1952 48

Plate 34 Excavations in the Cathedral Close, Exeter, in 1973 48

Plate 35 The Roman Fort at Okehampton 50

Plate 36 Excavations at the Roman Fort at Bolham, Tiverton 51

Plates 37, 38 The Axe Valley 52

Plate 39 Old Burrow, Countisbury 54

Plate 40 Possible Roman Signal Station or Fortlet near Exeter 55

Plate 41 Line of probable Roman Road at Colebrooke 56

Plate 42 A Romano-British Farm at Stoke Gabriel 57

Plates 43–48 Settlements known from cropmark evidence 58

Plate 49 Bantham Ham, South Devon 62

Plate 50 High Peak, East Devon 64

Plate 51 Lundy, Bristol Channel 65

Plate 52 Brent Tor, West Devon 66

Plate 53 Crediton Parish Church 67

Plate 54 The Anglo-Saxon *burh* at Lydford 68

Plate 55 Berry Camp, Branscombe 70

Plate 56 Roborough Castle, North Devon 71

Plate 57	Barnstaple	72
Plate 58	Loddiswell Rings	74
Plate 59	Holwell Castle, Parracombe	75
Plate 60	Okehampton Castle	76
Plate 61	Okehampton Park	77
Plate 62	South Hole, Hartland	78
Plate 63	Houndtor, Manaton, Dartmoor	79
Plate 64	Frithelstock Priory	80
Plate 65	Torre Abbey	81
Plate 66	South Molton	82
Plate 67	South Zeal	83
Plate 68	The Mouth of the River Dart	84
Plate 69	Dartmouth Castle	85
Plate 70	Greystone Bridge	86
Plate 71	Compton Castle, Marldon	87
Plate 72	Holcombe Rogus	88
Plate 73	Totnes	89
Plate 74	Bradworthy	90
Plate 75	Clovelly	91
Plate 76	Membury	92
Plate 77	Stokeinteignhead	92
Plate 78	Ugborough	93
Plate 79	Northlew	93
Plate 80	Plymouth Citadel	94
Plate 81	Braunton Great Field	96
Plate 82	Strip fields at Challacombe, Dartmoor	97
Plate 83	Combe Martin	98
Plate 84	Mediaeval and modern fields at Stockland	99
Plate 85	Sourton Down	100
Plate 86	Exeter Canal Basin and Quay	101
Plates 87–89	The Dartmoor Tin Industry	102
Plate 90	Agricultural Earthworks north of Tiverton	104
Plate 91	Tiverton from the east	105
Plate 92	Shobrooke Church and Barton	106
Plate 93	Haytor Quarry and Tramway	107
Plate 94	Powder Mills, Lydford	108
Plate 95	Canal at Bude	109
Plate 96	The Teign Estuary	110
Plate 97	Newquay, on the River Tamar	111
Plates 98–100	Clayworkings	112
Plate 101	Nineteenth-century Churches, St Marychurch, Torquay	114
Plate 102	Exe Vale Hospital, Exminster	115
Plate 103	Buckfast Abbey	116
Plate 104	Appledore Shipyards	117
Plate 105	Castle Drogo	118
Plate 106	Floods in the Exe and Culm Valleys	119
Plate 107	Landslips between Axmouth and Lyme Regis	120
Plate 108	Bridges across the Tamar	121
Plates 109, 110	Plymouth, from above the Hoe	122
Plates 111–114	The site of Roadford Reservoir, West Devon	124

Front cover: Clovelly Dykes hillfort *(F. M. Griffith, Devon County Council, 15 March 1985)*
Back cover: Braunton Great Field *(F. M. Griffith, Devon County Council, 18 December 1985)*

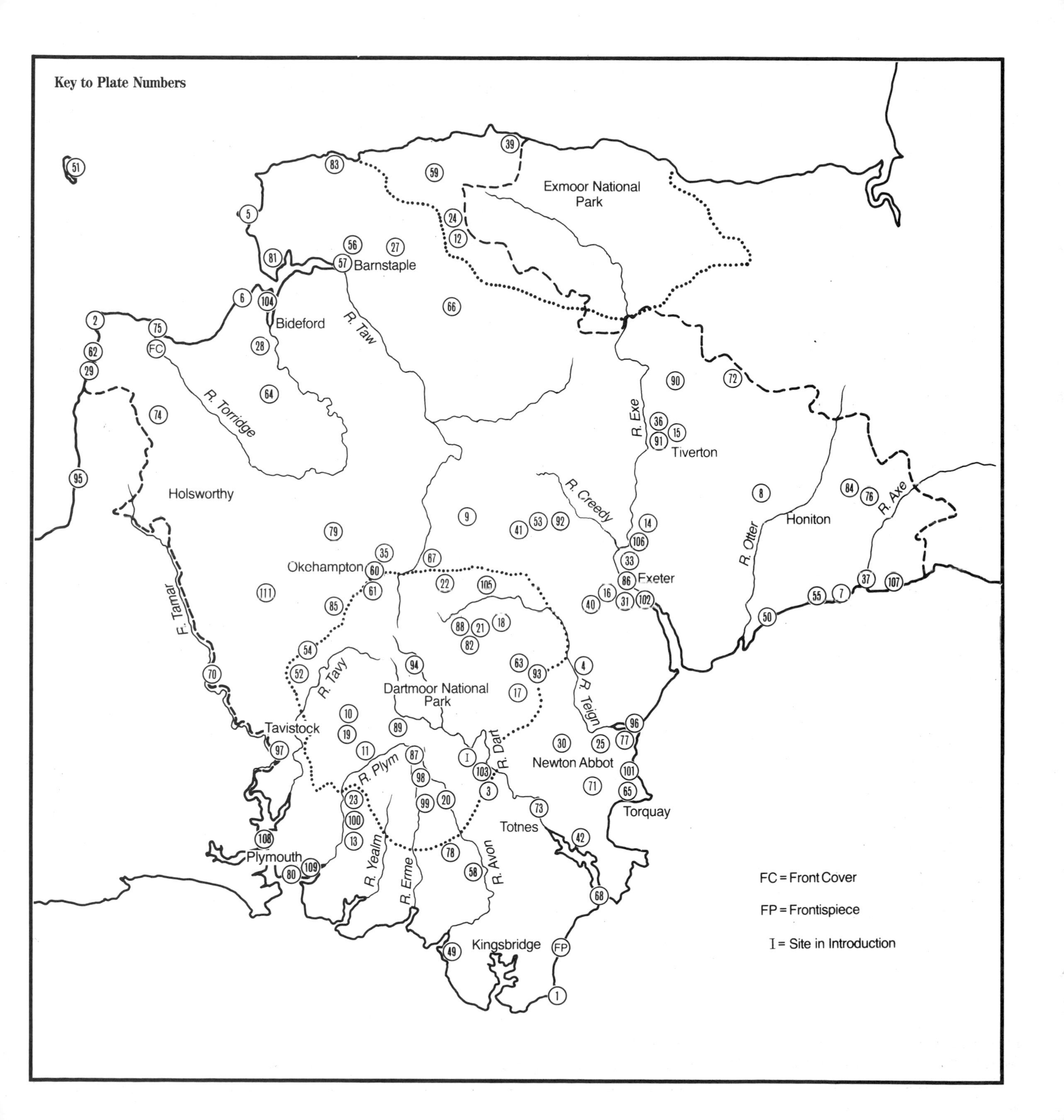
Key to Plate Numbers
Exmoor National Park
Barnstaple
Bideford
R. Taw
R. Torridge
Holsworthy
R. Exe
Tiverton
R. Creedy
R. Otter
Honiton
R. Axe
Okehampton
Exeter
R. Tamar
R. Tavy
Dartmoor National Park
R. Teign
Tavistock
R. Plym
R. Dart
Newton Abbot
Torquay
Totnes
Plymouth
R. Yealm
R. Erme
R. Avon
Kingsbridge
FC = Front Cover
FP = Frontispiece
I = Site in Introduction

Slapton Ley *A photograph from the Crawford Collection, taken on 19 June 1926*

INTRODUCTION

Devon is one of the largest counties in England, and one of the most varied in its geology and scenery. The county displays a corresponding wealth of variety in its archaeological and historical sites, which range from some of the earliest traces of palaeolithic activity in the country, through pastoral and agricultural settlements of many different periods, to monuments relating to Devon's industrial and maritime history. The aerial perspective can often provide a new insight into archaeological sites, even those which may be very familiar to us at ground level, and it also permits a more complete grasp of their topographical setting. Apart from recording known and upstanding monuments, aerial photography can also, by a number of methods which are outlined below, be the means of identifying previously unknown archaeological sites. This book has been written for the general reader to provide an introduction both to the various types of archaeological and historical monuments recorded from the air and to the current programme of aerial reconnaissance in the county. It is of course impossible to illustrate here more than a small proportion of the whole range of the county's archaeology: some of our most important and interesting sites have had to be omitted. It is, however, hoped that the selection presented will provide some indication of the richness and diversity of Devon's archaeological inheritance.

This is not the place to give a detailed account of Devon's archaeological and historical development. A number of books are available on the subject and a select bibliography is provided at the end of this introduction. The caption to each photograph gives a short description of the chief features shown and the reader is referred to the 'Further Reading' section at the end of each entry for more information on the significance and the detail of each site or topic. The sites presented in this book are arranged in broadly chronological order, but it will quickly become apparent to the reader that almost every picture illustrates a complex development of the landscape over many centuries, showing features dating from many different periods. This is one of the delights of the Devon landscape for the archaeologist, and one which aerial photography can demonstrate particularly well.

The Development of Aerial Archaeology

The earliest known aerial photograph of an archaeological site in Britain was of Stonehenge, taken from a military balloon tethered above Salisbury Plain in 1906. The Great War gave a considerable impetus to the development of aerial photographic techniques, and suggested to some wartime flyers the archaeological possibilities of air photography. These were to be the pioneers of archaeological aerial reconnaissance, most notably O.G.S. Crawford, the first Archaeology Officer of the Ordnance Survey, who had served in the RFC as an observer during the war. In the 1920s Crawford quickly involved others, at first mainly service pilots, in photographing archaeological sites. The story of the earliest work in this field is an absorbing one: the reader is referred to the bibliography at the end of this Introduction for books on the subject. The early aerial exploration of archaeological landscapes was centred on Wessex and the Oxford region – so often the heartland of the development of new archaeological methods. Little work was undertaken in the west of Britain at this time: the photograph of Slapton Ley which appears as the frontispiece to this book, not itself of a specifically archaeological subject, is one of the earliest surviving aerial photographs of Devon and was taken either by Crawford or under his auspices in 1926.

Crawford's first use of the aerial camera, in his study of the archaeology of Wessex in the 1920s, was to record the extensive prehistoric landscape then surviving in good condition on the chalk uplands, but he and others soon appreciated that, given certain ground conditions, the aerial observer could locate other types of site which were normally invisible or unidentifiable on the ground. The mechanisms by which this is possible are discussed below, but with this realization the process of aerial exploration of the landscape spread out beyond the chalk downlands of Wessex. First, work extended on to the river gravels of Oxfordshire, where the pioneering work of Major G.W.G. Allen was especially important, and then aerial photographers started to open up the archaeology of much of eastern England, examining areas which had been subjected to such vigorous cultivation that almost no traces of prehistoric activity had previously been known to survive, save in the durable form of flint artefacts. However, very little exploratory work was carried out in the west of England or in Wales in the inter-war period.

The Second World War resulted in both technical advances in cameras, films and aircraft and an increase in the numbers of those aware of the potential of aerial reconnaissance, much as the 1914–18 war had done. Another incidental benefit which derived from the great increase in aerial photographic activity was the large number of general reconnaissance photographs of the British countryside and towns taken during and immediately after the war, which provide a comprehensive record of the country at that time. Almost complete photographic coverage of Devon was achieved by the RAF in 1946–7 as part of the national air survey. The value of this record as a historical document increases year by year, as the pace of change in our landscape quickens.

Developments in Devon

In the immediate post-war period a number of new figures appeared on the archaeological aerial reconnaissance scene, many of whom were to have a profound impact on the development of the subject as well as expanding the range and scope of the activities of the aerial archaeologist. Of particular significance to Devon studies was the establishment of the Cambridge University Committee for Aerial Photography (CUCAP), under Dr (later Professor) J.K.S. St Joseph. Flying from Cambridge, Professor St Joseph was the first person to undertake regular archaeological reconnaissance flights over Devon, usually several times a year, and since the late 1940s the Cambridge Committee has built up, as part of its archive, the largest and most complete available collection of air photographs of Devon's archaeology. These have had a considerable impact on work in the county. All these photographs are available for public consultation in Cambridge; copies of some are also held at the County Sites and Monuments Register, and some of the

Cambridge photographs are reproduced in the present book.

As the importance of aerial photography to all branches of archaeology became increasingly appreciated, the Royal Commission on the Historical Monuments of England (RCHME) established its own Air Photographs Library, both to provide a central repository for the material by then being recorded by independent flyer-photographers working in various parts of the country and also to undertake its own programme of archaeological air photography. This Unit, established under the leadership of John Hampton, formed the other principal agency engaged in aerial reconnaissance over Devon, giving particular attention to the archaeology of Dartmoor.

While much archaeological information can be gained from air photographs taken for other or general survey purposes – and these are frequently used by archaeologists – it is the body of photography built up by these two agencies that formed the core of available work on the archaeology of Devon. Examination by the writer of all available material from these two bodies, especially the CUCAP photographs taken in the droughts of 1975 and 1976, demonstrated the clear potential for further and more concentrated reconnaissance in Devon. With the active encouragement and support of Professor St Joseph and his successor, David Wilson, at CUCAP, and of John Hampton at RCHME, trial sorties were flown by the writer with W.W. Dougan in 1983. These early ventures produced promising results (Griffith 1983). Further reconnaissance was carried out with funding from private sources in winter 1983–4 and in early summer 1984. The scale and significance of the results obtained in the early part of the 1984 drought in Devon prompted a large and rapid injection of funding into the project by HBMC (English Heritage) and Devon County Council, permitting some seventy hours of flying to be undertaken and resulting in the discovery of several hundred previously unrecorded archaeological sites, predominantly in lowland Devon (Griffith 1984). Since 1984 the project has received annual funding from English Heritage or RCHME and the survey is now integrated into the writer's regular archaeological work in Devon County Council.

Fig. 1 A very slight hilltop enclosure in north-west Devon, recorded in low oblique sunlight.
Photograph: F. M. Griffith, Devon County Council, 22 December 1986

Air Photography and Archaeology

Mapping

Air photography has a multitude of uses for the archaeologist and the student of the landscape. The purely illustrative function has been touched on above; its value is demonstrated by some of the following photographs. The perception of an ancient site, townscape, or building can be substantially enhanced by an appreciation of the aerial view. For some sites, such as High Peak (plate 50), the air view is the only practical way to see the monument as a whole! The historical development of a town such as Barnstaple (plate 57) can be appreciated more clearly from an air photograph than from any other visual guide, as can the layout of a complicated modern building such as Exe Vale Hospital (plate 102). The aerial perspective can also be of great benefit when dealing with an extensive landscape or difficult terrain: nowadays primary mapping of remote parts of the world is generally carried out using photogrammetric plots of air photographs as the first stage in the mapping process. The revision of Ordnance Survey maps in Britain also makes a considerable use of air photographs. In our own region, the mapping of the extensive multiperiod archaeological landscapes of Exmoor and Dartmoor has long created problems for the archaeologist, and the use of air photographs can transform the work of the surveyor.

While air-photo transcription cannot always offer the subtlety of recording or the analytical skills of the experienced field surveyor, in the right hands air photographs can provide an outline map of an upstanding archaeological landscape far more quickly than ground survey can. The utility of air photographs for such work depends on the quality and availability of the photographs and the time of year and of day at which they were taken. There is also a problem in that some classes of archaeological site, such as extensive field systems (for example, plate 17), will by their nature show better on air photos and therefore the resulting map than small or slight monuments, and thus information derived from air photographs has to be used with circumspection in considering the total archaeological picture. Nevertheless, both by giving an overall view of a landscape whose vegetation or terrain may make field survey difficult and fragmented, and through the inherent economy of the technique of air-photo transcription as compared with primary field survey, such work can be an invaluable tool for the first stages of a complete archaeological survey which can then be amplified, corrected and enhanced by a subsequent field programme. Such a project has recently been carried out for Bodmin Moor in Cornwall (Johnson 1985; RCHME forthcoming [a]) and a similar but less intensive piece of work to produce a sketch-plotted map of Dartmoor has recently been undertaken by RCHME in conjunction with the Devon Sites and Monuments Register and English Heritage (RCHME forthcoming [b]), providing for the first time mapping of the visible archaeology of the moor to a common scale. For Exmoor, similar work has been produced by R. McDonnell (DCC 1981).

Shadow sites and soilmarks

In an area such as Dartmoor we may use aerial photography principally to map archaeological features whose existence we can both verify and indeed discover by the normal methods of ground survey. This is, however, not always the case. Even where features such as field banks or reaves (see p.32) can afterwards be observed on the ground, problems of the terrain may prevent their initial recognition in ground survey because they appear in broken up and meaningless fragments. Only by drawing back, as it were, to a distance, can we appreciate the picture as a whole. On other occasions a feature may be genuinely so slight that it can only be observed at all in very favourable lighting conditions. Usually this means conditions of oblique sunlight, such as that of early morning and late evening in summer or throughout the day in midwinter, so that the shadow cast by a slight earthwork is as pronounced as possible. Sometimes earthworks can be recorded in this way which are so slight that they are almost invisible in the field, even to one aware of their existence. Fig. 1 is a good example of such an earthwork: this site is barely perceptible on the ground. Reconnaissance for sites of this sort has to be well planned, and carried out at many different times of day (especially in a county like Devon where relatively little of the ground is flat, so that sites on hillslopes will be perceptible only in oblique light from one direction). These sites are known as 'shadow sites': other examples can be seen in plates 27, 30 and 90.

Shadow sites often represent the last upstanding traces of an earthwork which is in the process of disappearing altogether, either through natural erosion or because of agricultural operations. We know from the archaeological record that this is not a new phenomenon – there are instances of ploughed-out prehistoric sites discovered beneath excavated Roman ones, for example – but nevertheless in recent years the pace of erosion of sites by cultivation processes has noticeably increased. It has been estimated, for example, that in the Cotswolds, out of 237 Bronze Age barrows surviving after the last war only ninety-five have not suffered damage from cultivation – thus as much damage has probably been done in the last forty years as in the previous 4000. Sites in a state of active erosion by cultivation can be observed from the air in certain circumstances as 'soilmarks', as in fig. 2: this enclosure's bank was made of subsoil dug from its ditch, which therefore shows as lighter in colour than the surrounding topsoil of the field. While archaeological sites can certainly be discovered in this way, a soilmark like this is distressing to the archaeologist, since such a mark will show only when a site is under active erosion, for example by ploughing, and after a while the differing soil colours will be mixed together by further ploughing. A soilmark of this sort therefore shows the active destruction of previously surviving archaeological deposits.

The term 'soilmark' is also used for a rather different kind of mark observable from the air. These are sometimes called 'dampmarks', although they can be caused by differential conditions of either moisture or heat. A buried deposit or feature such as a ditch will often have different moisture- or heat-retaining characteristics from the surrounding subsoil, and in some weather conditions this will give a clue to a site's existence by outlining the buried feature, either as a moist mark in an otherwise dry ploughed field, or as a mark where frost has melted before that on the rest of the field due to the greater warmth-retaining character of the underlying deposits, or by the converse of either of these processes.

Frost and snow can also help to identify very low earthworks which would normally be virtually invisible. In the case of an even cover of snow or frost

Fig. 2 A small rectilinear enclosure visible as a soilmark soon after ploughing.
Photograph: F. M. Griffith, Devon County Council, 18 February 1987

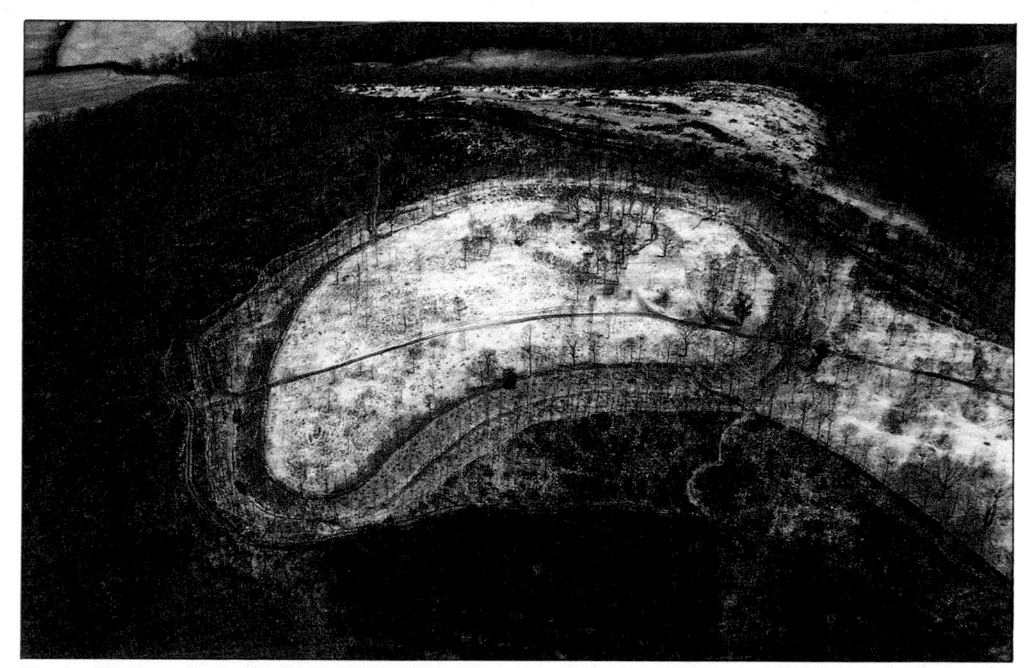

Fig. 3 Hembury Castle, Buckfastleigh, under snow: a Norman motte within a prehistoric hillfort. (Since this photograph was taken the interior of the hillfort has been cleared of trees.)
Photograph: F. M. Griffith, Devon County Council, 20 March 1987

over a field, the sun will melt the cover of the sunward side of low earthworks before the rest, leaving them outlined as bare marks in an otherwise white field. Conversely, the side of the bank left in shadow will be the last part of the field for the frost to melt, and so this will appear as a white mark in a bare field. Very slight ditches and depressions will also keep snow from melting longer – the slight dips of the cultivation ridges in plate 85 are a good example of this phenomenon. In some special conditions, snow can allow one to distinguish sites in woodland which cannot be seen from the air at any other time. The photograph (fig. 3) of the hillfort and Norman motte at Hembury Castle, Buckfastleigh shows this well.

Cropmarks

Buried archaeological features such as ditches and pits are often filled with a different material from the subsoil into which they are cut. This is after all the way they are identified during the process of archaeological excavation. As outlined above, the differential moisture- and warmth-retaining qualities of these buried deposits can reveal their presence in winter. The same phenomenon can be exploited in some circumstances in summer. In a drought, where the moisture content of the topsoil and subsoil is insufficient to provide for all the requirements of a growing crop, a buried feature (whether made by natural or human agency) cut into the subsoil may provide better moisture retention than the subsoil and hence permit a crop to grow more vigorously where that feature is located. On the other hand, a buried wall or other impermeable structure will cause premature parching of the crop above it. In either case, the outline of the underlying features will be temporarily mirrored in the growing crop.

Fig. 4 illustrates this point, and a typical Devon 'cropmark', as the growth patterns resulting from such a process are known, is shown in figs 5 and 6. In the first, the cropmark is visible as a denser green mark in the growing crop in the moister conditions above a buried ditch, while in the second picture, of the same site, part of the crop is ripening but the plants above the buried feature are remaining green longer, as well as showing greater height and density of growth. The next step in this sequence is for an unripe cropmark to be visible in a ripe crop (as in plate 9), and lastly, stronger denser growth will sometimes continue to betray the presence of a buried site in a fully ripened crop. (It should be said that these marks will also be visible on the ground: the use of an aircraft is not essential for their recognition but will permit the observer to understand their significance more readily.)

In practice cropmark formation is more complex than this might suggest, and there are many other factors affecting it. For example, the phenomenon will

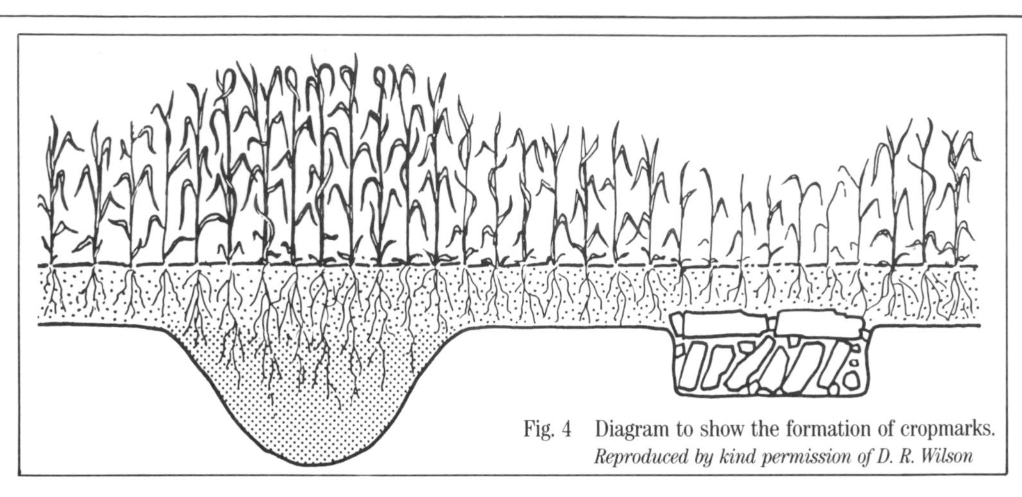

Fig. 4 Diagram to show the formation of cropmarks.
Reproduced by kind permission of D. R. Wilson

Fig. 5 (and Fig. 6) The same site illustrates two different stages in the development of a cropmark.

occur only when a crop is actively growing and demanding moisture, and some sorts of crop are much more sensitive to crop stress and hence to cropmark production than others. Different crops have different growing seasons, and so the timing of a period of drought will dictate the crops on which it will have any effect at all – buried sites underlying other crops may remain entirely invisible and undiscovered. It will also be understood that the whole process of cropmark production depends on the *difference* between the buried feature and its immediate surroundings, and this difference is likely to occur more quickly and more often on a light free-draining subsoil than on a heavy soil with good moisture-retaining characteristics. This is why we know of more sites that have been recorded as cropmarks on the light soils of the river valleys of our area than on the heavier soils of, for example, the Culm Measures. In most summers a few cropmarks will appear on the lighter soils, but a drought like that of 1984 can show these sites in their hundreds and also reveal them on the heavier soils. Again, the depth of soil may vary across a field, so part of a site will be clearly seen as a cropmark while the rest remains obscure.

A further complication in examining the overall pattern of cropmark occurrence is that different areas of Devon have different proportions under cultivation with those crops which are prone to produce cropmarks. The amount of rainfall in a particular area will also affect the likelihood of cropmarks being visible, and the volume and distribution of annual rainfall varies considerably in different parts of the country. Again, at any given time a high proportion of the west of Britain is under a crop of grass, which will only produce cropmarks at all under exceptional conditions of late summer drought (when, however, they can be very clear). The result of the combination of all these factors is that south-west England does not produce cropmarks as readily or as frequently as many of the more eastern parts of the country. For this reason, and because of the relatively small amount of regular aerial reconnaissance in the county, Devon was long regarded not only as difficult terrain for cropmark production, but indeed as being without the sites whose partially destroyed remains the cropmarks represent.

These factors have in the past resulted in an underestimate of the density of early settlement, particularly for the prehistoric period. When the relative absence of upstanding sites on the lowland, long cultivated, parts of Devon has been compared with the abundance of surviving archaeological remains on the upland areas such as Dartmoor, it has often led to the belief that prehistoric people must preferentially have occupied the upland. It is only in comparatively recent years that increased and more intensive aerial observation of the lowlands, not only of Devon but other parts of western England and Wales as well, coupled with more intensive fieldwalking techniques, has started to redress this balance and give us perhaps a more realistic impression of the prehistoric settlement pattern of our area.

Enormous problems remain in the way of this attempt by archaeologists to reconstruct the 'real' settlement pattern; the factors affecting discovery, as outlined above, are so many and varied that a long programme of work is necessary to get anything like a true picture even of those sites that will produce marks at all. The problem for the archaeologist is to work out whether there were really more prehistoric settlements on the light soils with sensitive crops, or whether the pattern is entirely the product of the differential visibility of the sites. (The answer appears to be a combination of the two.) One may also observe that the recording of these sites at all is dependent upon the aerial archaeologist being in the right place at the right time: fig. 7 illustrates that cropmarks wait for no one!

Furthermore, this technique is generally applicable only to cultivated ground, and then only to the identification of enclosed sites – those which show up by reason of their enclosure ditch. We know from excavation that many settlement sites of past periods were not in fact demarcated in this way, their houses and other structures being either completely unenclosed or protected by an ephemeral feature such as a wattle fence. Such settlements will be almost invisible to the aerial observer, especially on the heavier soils of this region, and the use of information derived from aerial photography will always be only one technique

Fig. 6. *Photographs: F. M. Griffith, Devon County Council, 3 July 1985 and 23 July 1985*

to be exploited in conjunction with many others, such as field survey, geophysical survey, historical evidence, and field collection of artefacts. Nevertheless, the impact of aerial reconnaissance on the understanding of past settlement patterns has been as dramatic in Devon and the west of Britain in the last decade as the application of the same technique was in the gravel heartlands of Oxfordshire in the 1920s and 1930s. The results of aerial reconnaissance in the study of the scale and distribution of evidence of human activity other than settlement sites – for example, prehistoric ceremonial sites – has been equally great, as some of the following photographs will demonstrate.

The study of the various processes by which archaeological sites may be recognized through the medium of plant growth is a complicated and continuing one, with almost infinite subtleties and refinements which depend upon the plant species and variety, the season, the rate of climatic change and many other factors hardly touched upon in the brief summary above. For a more detailed discussion of all these issues the reader is referred to the books on the subject listed at the end of this Introduction.

Fig. 7 The aerial archaeologist must be in the right place at the right time in order to record cropmarks.
Photograph: F. M. Griffith, Devon County Council, 7 July 1984

SELECT BIBLIOGRAPHY

The Archaeology and History of Devon

Beacham, P.M. (ed.) *Devon Building* (Devon Books, 1989)
Durrance, E.M. and Laming, D.J.C. (eds) *The Geology of Devon* (University of Exeter, 1982)
Devon County Council (ed. S.C. Timms) *Archaeology of the Devon Landscape* (1980)
Fox, A. *South West England 3500 BC – AD 600* (David & Charles, 2nd ed. 1973)
Hoskins, W.G. *Devon* (1954, new ed. David & Charles, 1972)
Pearce, S.M. *The Archaeology of South West Britain* (Collins, 1981)
Pevsner, N. *The Buildings of England: North Devon* and *South Devon* (2 vols), (Penguin, 1952; 2nd edition, by B. Cherry, forthcoming 1989)
Stanes, R. *A History of Devon* (Phillimore, 1986)
Timms, S.C. (ed) *Archaeology of the Devon Landscape* (new ed. Devon Books, 1989)
Todd, M. *The South-West to AD 1000* (Longman, 1987)

The Development of Aerial Archaeology

Allen, G.W.G. 1984 *Discovery from the Air (Aerial Archaeology* vol. 10)
Bradford, J. *Ancient Landscapes: Studies in Field Archaeology* (Greenwood Press, 1980)
Crawford, O.G.S. 'Air Survey and Archaeology', *Geographical Journ.* (May 1923, 324 – 66)
— *Air Survey and Archaeology* (Ordnance Survey Professional Papers 7, 1928)
— and Keiller, A. *Wessex from the Air* (Clarendon Press, 1928)
Deuel, L. *Flights into Yesterday* (Penguin, 1971)
Riley, D. *Air Photography and Archaeology* (Duckworth, 1987)
St Joseph, J.K.S. (ed.) *The Uses of Air Photography* (Black, 1977, 2nd ed.)

Recent Work in Aerial Archaeology

Maxwell, G.S. *The Impact of Aerial Reconnaissance on Archaeology* (CBA Res. Rep. 49, 1983)
Wilson, D.R. *Aerial Reconnaissance for Archaeology* (CBA Res. Rep. 12, 1975)
— *Air Photo Interpretation for Archaeologists* (Batsford, 1982)
The journal *Aerial Archaeology* is devoted to new work in the subject, and a number of new developments are regularly published in the quarterly *Antiquity*.
Recent work in Devon is described under the appropriate entries in the text.

Archaeological Sites from the Air

Some of the work of the Cambridge University Committee for Air Photography has been published in thematic volumes in the series *Cambridge Air Surveys:*
Knowles, D. and St Joseph, J.K.S. *Monastic Sites from the Air* (Cambridge University Press, 1952)
Beresford, M.W. and St Joseph, J.K.S. *Medieval England. An Aerial Survey* (Cambridge University Press, 1958, 2nd ed. 1979)
Norman, E.R. and St Joseph, J.K.S. 1969 *The Early Development of Irish Society* (Cambridge University Press, 1969)
Frere, S.S. and St Joseph, J.K.S. *Roman Britain from the Air* (Cambridge University Press, 1983)
Photographs from the Cambridge collection are also used in:
Muir, R. *History from the Air* (Michael Joseph 1983, new ed. 1987)

Closer to home, aerial photographs from a number of sources appear with a descriptive text and interpretative overlays in Greeves, T.A.P. *The Archaeology of Dartmoor from the Air* (Devon Books, 1985).

References in the Introduction

DCC 1981: Devon County Council *Archaeology in Devon: Annual Report no 4, 1980–81*, 28–9
Griffith, F.M. 1983 'The Identification of four enclosure sites north of Teignmouth', *PDAS* 41, 63–8
— 1984 'Aerial reconnaissance in Devon in 1984' *PDAS* 42, 7–10
Johnson, N. 'The results of air and ground survey on Bodmin Moor, Cornwall' in (ed.) Maxwell, G.S. (1983) (above).
RCHME (forthcoming) (a) *Bodmin Moor, an Aerial and Ground Survey, vol 1: The Prehistoric and Historic Landscape* (produced in conjunction with the Cornwall Archaeological Unit).
RCHME (forthcoming) (b) *Dartmoor. An Air Photographic Survey.*

Further Reading

Under most of the entries for individual sites, references are given for further reading. These are not intended to be exhaustive, but to direct the reader to a fuller account of the subject and further information on each site. Names of books are given in full, but in the case of articles published in journals the title of the journal is given in abbreviated form. The abbreviations used are:

Antiq. J. – The Antiquaries' Journal
Archaeol. J. – Archaeological Journal
Arch. Review – Architectural Review
Devon Archaeol. – Devon Archaeology
Med. Archaeol. – Medieval Archaeology
PDAS – Proceedings of the Devon Archaeological Society
PMMCJ – Plymouth Mineral and Mining Club Journal
PPS – Proceedings of the Prehistoric Society
TDA – Transactions of the Devonshire Association
TTNHS – Transactions and Proceedings of the Torquay Natural History Society

Information on sites illustrated here is also derived from the County Sites and Monuments Register, maintained by Devon County Council at County Hall. This archive also contains most of the air photographs from the RAF 1946–7 survey, copies of many photographs from the Cambridge and RCHME collections, and those taken in the more recent Devon survey project. The Sites and Monuments Register may be consulted by members of the public by prior appointment (telephone Exeter 272266).

Other abbreviations used in references are:

BAR – British Archaeological Reports, British Series or International Series
CBA – Council for British Archaeology Research Report series
DAS – Devon Archaeological Society
DBG – Devon Buildings Group
EAR – Exeter Archaeological Reports
EPNS – English Place-Name Society
ESH – Exeter Studies in History
IGS – Institute of Geological Sciences
MVRG – Medieval Village Research Group
OUCA – Oxford University Committee for Archaeology Monograph Series

THE SITES ILLUSTRATED IN THIS BOOK

The photographs in this book have been chosen to show something of the range of the riches of Devon's archaeology and history, interpreting these terms in the widest sense. It is hoped that their diversity will serve to remind readers of the wealth of Devon's resources in such material, but at the same time of the essential fragility of much that is shown. Outside the towns, readers are asked to remember that the archaeological sites illustrated are in the main on private land: apart from the unenclosed land on Dartmoor and Exmoor there is unlikely to be any right of access to the sites without the landowner's permission. In addition, almost all the archaeological sites shown here are protected by law as Scheduled Ancient Monuments of national importance, which means that it is a criminal offence to disturb them in any way, or to use a metal detector on them, without the consent of the Secretary of State.

ACKNOWLEDGEMENTS

The development of the recent programme of air survey in Devon has been due to the help and support of many institutions and individuals. The commitment of Devon County Council members and officers has been important, while the costs of the flying have in the main been met by DCC and by generous grant aid from the Department of the Environment (latterly English Heritage) and from the Royal Commission on the Historical Monuments of England. Prior to this, the Devon project received financial help from Mrs A.M. Griffith, Mrs C.A. Richards, Miss H. Smith and The Devonshire Association. For practical and moral support throughout I am most grateful to Professor J.K.S. St Joseph and Mr David Wilson of Cambridge, to Mr John Hampton and Dr Rowan Whimster of RCHME, to the members of the Council for British Archaeology's Aerial Archaeology Committee, and to members of the Devonshire Association and the Devon Archaeological Society. Above all my thanks are due to my colleague Simon Timms of Devon County Council and to my pilot, Mr W.W. Dougan of Exeter Flying Club, for their unfailing co-operation and enthusiasm for the project.

For the printing of the photographs I should like to thank the staff of DCC's photographic section, of RCHME Air Photographs Library, of the Cambridge Committee for Aerial Photography, of Exeter City Museums, and John Saunders and members of the University of Exeter Photographic Department. In the preparation of the text I have benefited from discussions with and help from John Allan, Peter Berridge, Piran Bishop, Dr Mark Brayshay, Dr Jo Cox, Dr Tom Greeves, Chris Henderson, Dr Robert Higham, Michael Laithwaite, Norah Luxton, Henrietta and Norman Quinnell, Rosemary Robinson, Win Scutt, Simon Timms, Peter Weddell and Major Freddy Woodward. Errors and omissions remain my own.

I would also like to offer my especial thanks to the owners of many of the sites illustrated here for their almost unfailing welcome and hospitality, and their interest in the sites on their land. Farmers' knowledge of the land will practically always expand and give context to the information available from the air photograph itself, while their interest in the archaeological monuments in their care is the surest guarantee of the sites' well-being. To all these owners, and to those of many other sites not shown here, I am most grateful.

Photographs are reproduced here by permission of the Royal Commission on the Historical Monuments of England, the Cambridge University Committee for Aerial Photography, Exeter City Council, Plymouth City Council, South West Water, the Central Excavation Unit of English Heritage and Devon Archaeological Society.

Other photographs are by Devon County Council and the author. All copyright reserved.

The map on p. v is by Ian Foulis and Associates. The line drawings are by Sandy Morris of Exeter City Museums Archaeological Field Unit.

Plate 1

Start Point

Devon's name is perhaps best known worldwide as the name of a whole system of geological time. The term 'Devonian system' was first used in 1839 by the Rev. Adam Sedgwick and Sir Roderick Murchison in a paper to the British Association for the Advancement of Science to describe a series of marine rocks, broadly contemporary with the Old Red Sandstone and underlying the strata of the Carboniferous Era. Here at Start Point, on Devon's south-east coast, the Lower and Middle Devonian schists outcrop, providing a view of some of the oldest rocks in Devon, thought to be between 350 and 400 million years old.

This view is taken from the south, looking up the coast towards Berry Head. The freshwater lagoon of Slapton Ley can just be made out in the middle distance. On Start Point itself, extensive flint scatters provide evidence for human activity here throughout the prehistoric period from the Mesolithic onwards.

The lighthouse at Start Point is notable in having been the last in Britain to be built, in 1837, under patent from Trinity House. The patent system was one whereby the contract for the construction was let out to a private entrepreneur. Results were found to be so variable that after this Trinity House, the national organization that looks after lighthouses and lightships, assumed direct responsibility for construction. The lighthouse at Start Point is said to occupy one of the most exposed situations on the British mainland.

Further Reading

Durrance, E.M. and Laming, D.J.C. *The Geology of Devon* (University of Exeter, 1982)

Jackson, D. *Lighthouses of England and Wales* (David & Charles, 1975)

Sedgwick, A. and Murchison, R.I. 'Classification of the Older Stratified Rocks of Devon and Cornwall', *London and Edinburgh Philosophical Magazine and Journal of Science* 14 (1839), 241–60

Photograph: F.M. Griffith, Devon County Council, 18 February 1987

Plate 2

Cliffs at Hartland Point, North-west Devon

At the opposite extremity of the county, at Hartland in north-west Devon, the coastal scenery is of a very different sort. The aerial photograph gives an excellent illustration of the character of the cliffs at Hartland: here the interbedded sandstones and shales of the Crackington Formation of the Culm Measures are spectacularly folded, so that in places the bedding planes of the rocks lie almost vertically. Below the cliffs the varied rock strata provide a colourful range of pebbles.

Steep cliffs like these continue from Hartland Point (to the left of this picture) south for almost 30 km. The coast here is hostile to the sailor and offers no really safe harbours between Boscastle to the south and Bideford, 30 km the other side of Hartland Point on the River Torridge. The harbour at Clovelly, on the north coast of the Hartland peninsula, was constructed in the late sixteenth century, but is not secure in all weathers, while Hartland Quay, built at around the same time, is even less so. Bude Haven, closer than Boscastle to the south, was until its improvement in 1818 (see plate 95) 'small and Difficult of entry', according to the surveyor James Green.

Further Reading

Edmonds, E.A. *Classification of Carboniferous Rocks of South West England* (IGS Report 74/13, 1974)

Pearse Chope, R. *The Book of Hartland* (Devonshire Press, 1940)

Photograph: J.K.S. St Joseph, Cambridge University, 29 June 1948

Plate 3

Higher Kiln Quarry, Buckfastleigh

Buckfastleigh lies on the Devonian limestone, and the hill on which the parish church (right of picture) is situated is honeycombed with a complex system of caves formed by solution of the limestone. Higher Kiln Quarry, on the left of the picture, cuts into the cave system: during quarrying operations the caves were found to contain the remains of extinct Pleistocene animals probably dating from the last interglacial before the last Ice Age. These included bison, straight-tusked elephant, hyaena and hippopotamus, but unlike the very important Pleistocene cave site at Kent's Cavern, Torquay, no traces of human activity in the caves have ever been found. Joint Mitnor Cave and others at Buckfastleigh are now designated Sites of Special Scientific Interest, and Joint Mitnor is now in the care of the William Pengelly Cave Studies Trust.

Buckfastleigh church stands high on the hill a little way from the town. The fabric dates mainly from the thirteenth to fifteenth centuries. Outside the south door a small square building can be seen: this houses the seventeenth-century tomb of the notorious Richard Cabell, upon whose story Conan Doyle is said to have based *The Hound of the Baskervilles*.

At the top of the picture a small roofless building stands in the churchyard. This is not the predecessor of the parish church, as has sometimes been suggested, but a separate chapel, probably a chantry, dating from the late twelfth century.

Further Reading

Sutcliffe, A.J. 'Joint Mitnor Cave', *TTNHS* 13 pt 1 (1960), 1–26

Caves in Buckfastleigh Quarries (William Pengelly Cave Studies Trust Occasional Publication 1, 1979)

Photograph: F.M. Griffith, Devon County Council, 11 January 1988

Plate 4

Chudleigh Caves

Chudleigh (the village can be seen top left) also lies on the Devonian limestone, and much has also been quarried here. Where the Kate Brook (centre of picture) has cut a little gorge through the limestone, the caves, again formed by solution of the limestone, have been found to contain archaeological deposits. In contrast with Joint Mitnor Cave at Buckfastleigh, however, the Chudleigh caves contain both Pleistocene animal remains and evidence of the use of the caves by humans: flint tools from some of the caves indicate Middle and Upper Palaeolithic (Old Stone Age) activity, whilst the bone remains suggest animals from both cold and temperate phases of the Pleistocene.

On top of the left-hand side of the gorge is the site of the Chudleigh palace of the mediaeval bishops of Exeter. Only incomplete fragments of walling remain above ground, but extensive earthworks survive to indicate the former size of the palace.

Note Not only are the sites mentioned above protected as Scheduled Ancient Monuments, but access to the caves is now shut off as they are an important bat roost. Visitors should not approach the caves in case they disturb the bats.

Further Reading

Beynon, F. 'The Cow Cave, Chudleigh', *TTNHS* 6 (1934), 127–32

Collcutt, S.N. 'The Later Upper Palaeolithic Site of Pixies' Hole, Chudleigh, South Devon' in (ed.) Collcutt, S.N. *The Palaeolithic of Britain and Northern France: Recent Trends* (J.R. Collis, 1986), 73–4

Pengelly, W. 'The Ossiferous Cavern and Fissures in the Neighbourhood of Chudleigh, Devon', *TDA* 6 (1873), 46–60

Photograph: F.M. Griffith, Devon County Council, 18 February 1987

Plate 5

Baggy Point, Georgeham

Baggy Point projects into the Bristol Channel north of the Taw–Torridge estuary. It is formed from sedimentary slates and sandstones of the Upper Devonian series, and is now the property of the National Trust. Since the last century large quantities of flint and chert artefacts have been recovered in the vicinity of Baggy Point, allowing us to appreciate the extent of activity in the area in the prehistoric period. Collections from this headland are to be found in many Devon museums – a particularly large group of flint tools is in the Royal Albert Memorial Museum in Exeter – and as far afield as the Ashmolean Museum in Oxford. Most of this material dates from the Later Mesolithic period (6800–3500 b.c. in radiocarbon years), much of it in the form of the characteristic artefacts known as microliths – small worked flint pieces that served as projectile points and as parts of complex tools. While the Mesolithic period was a long one, and we cannot date most of these occupation sites with precision within the period, the extent of the flint scatters and their density suggest that this area, together with much of present-day coastal north Devon, was an important source of food and raw materials (for example, flint from the beaches) for mesolithic people.

At that time the sea level was considerably lower than today, as more sea water was still frozen into the polar ice at the end of the last glaciation. Consequently, the coastline was further out into what is now the Bristol Channel – probably at about the level of the modern 10 fathom submarine contour – and the channel itself was more like a broad estuary between north Devon and Wales. At the time of its exploitation by mesolithic people (probably itinerant rather than living in settled year-round sites), Baggy Point would therefore not have lain directly on the coast.

Further Reading

Gardner, K. 'A Mesolithic Survey of North Devon', *TDA* 89 (1957), 160–74

Grinsell, L.V. *The Archaeology of Exmoor* (David & Charles, 1970), 15–21

Jacobi, R. 'Early Flandrian Hunters in the South-West', *PDAS* 37 (1979), 48–93

Wymer, J.J. *Gazetteer of Mesolithic Sites* (CBA Res. Rep. 20, 1977)

Photograph: F.M. Griffith, Devon County Council, 7 January 1988

Plate 6

Westward Ho!

Also on Devon's north coast lies this important site off Westward Ho! Like Baggy Point, this has been known from finds for many years as an area occupied in the Mesolithic period, but, being more low-lying than Baggy Point, it is usually under water and can only be investigated at particularly low tides. The site was probably once more extensive: in recent years it has suffered considerable erosion by the sea and is now almost all lost. The archaeological deposits at Westward Ho! are found within a complex sequence of marine clay deposits, peats and other vegetation, including the stumps of substantial trees. Such 'submerged forests' have been recorded in many places around the coast of Devon and Cornwall and bear witness to the greater land area of the peninsula in this period.

Extensive evidence for mesolithic activity has been recovered from this site over the last 100 years. Recently, rescue excavations in response to the erosion of the site have involved systematic scientific recording of the surviving remains and extensive laboratory analysis. The recent work has also clarified the fact, missed by previous researchers, that submerged deposits of several different dates are preserved here, including evidence not only for mesolithic activity but also neolithic and Romano-British phases of exploitation.

A little further east, organic material similar to that from Westward Ho!, including bones, leaves and hazelnut shells, was recently discovered preserved in the anaerobic clays of the river bed during construction of the bridge taking the new route of the A39 road across the River Torridge. It is possible that this may represent traces of mesolithic activity, perhaps comparable with that at the Westward Ho! site, on the bank of the river as it then was and subsequently buried in marine clays when the sea level rose.

(The village of Westward Ho!, incidentally, did not exist at all until the mid nineteenth century. It was built by speculative developers after the publication of Charles Kingsley's book of that name.)

Further Reading

Balaam, N.D. *et al* 'Prehistoric and Romano-British Sites at Westward Ho! Devon: Archaeological and Palaeoenvironmental Surveys 1983 and 1984' in (ed.) Balaam, N.D. *et al. Studies in Palaeoeconomy and Environment in South West England* (BAR Brit. Ser. 181, 1987), 163–264

Churchill, D.M. 'The Kitchen-Midden site at Westward Ho!, Devon, England: Ecology, age, and relation to changes in land and sea levels', *PPS* 31 (1965), 74–84

Griffith, F.M. *et al* 'Submerged Deposits at Torridge Bridge', *PDAS* forthcoming

Jacobi, R. 'Early Flandrian Hunters in the South-West', *PDAS* 37 (1979), 48–93

Rogers, E.H. 'The raised Beach, Submerged Forest and Kitchen Midden of Westward Ho! and the Submerged Stone Row of Yelland', *PDAS* 3 (1946), 109–35

Photograph: F.M. Griffith, 14 August 1983

Plate 7

Beer Head

Beer Head represents the most westerly extent of the Cretaceous chalk and Greensand ridge that stretches south-west across England from Norfolk through Wiltshire to Devon. At Beer the chalk outcrops in the cliffs, capped by a layer of clay-with-flints. The site of Beer Head and the surrounding cliffs along Devon's south-east coast were of considerable importance in the earlier prehistoric period as the source of the best quality flint for the manufacture of artefacts such as arrowheads. While chert – a substance chemically closely related to flint but not so well suited to the production of fine-quality tools by knapping – occurs in the Greensand deposits of east Devon and the Haldon Ridge, and flint is found in the form of pebbles in beach deposits along Devon's north and south coasts, the flint from Beer has always been the finest readily available in south-west England. Particularly in the Neolithic period, Beer flint travelled long distances westward down the peninsula. We do not know whether this resulted from direct gathering of the flint by its ultimate users or whether a more complex network of trading patterns existed. In contrast to what has been suggested in the past, there is no evidence of actual mining of flint in the prehistoric period at Beer, and it is more probable that fresh exposures of the flint beds in the constantly eroding cliff face were exploited.

The thin soils above the chalk on top of Beer Head preserve the remains of small squarish fields with strongly lynchetted banks, similar to the well-known 'Celtic' (later prehistoric) fields of Wessex. Some of these can be seen in the photograph, and their survival here and in the Torquay area (see page 45), where cultivation of the very thin topsoil cover of the fields has been limited, suggests that fields such as these may previously have been quite common in lowland Devon, in spite of their rarity now.

Further Reading

Bordaz. J. *Tools of the Old and New Stone Age* (1959, British ed. David & Charles, 1970)

Pitts, M. *Later Stone Implements* (Shire Publications, 1980)

Photograph: F.M. Griffith, 29 October 1983

Plate 8

Hembury Hillfort, Payhembury

One of Devon's most striking hillforts, Hembury occupies a spur of the Greensand plateau of east Devon. The location provides a site of great natural strength: this photograph, taken from the south, shows how the naturally steep slopes have been further fortified by banks and ditches. Across the neck of the spur (top of picture), where access to the site is least difficult, the defences have been even more strongly built and still have a height of some 10 m between rampart top and ditch bottom.

The earthworks we see today date from the Iron Age occupation of the hilltop, but excavations in the 1920s and 1930s by Miss D. Liddell for Devon Archaeological Exploration Society, and in the 1980s by Professor Todd of Exeter University (whose excavation trench is visible in the centre of the hillfort), have shown that Hembury has a much longer history. It was first occupied in the Mesolithic period, and then, in the earlier Neolithic period (in the fourth millennium B.C.), it was the site of an important defended enclosure, a causewayed ditch and bank protecting the end of the spur. There may also have been other neolithic enclosures on the hilltop.

The hillfort itself was probably built in the earlier first millennium B.C. Its close-set multiple ramparts and hilltop siting are features characteristic of southern British hillforts, but sites like this are found only in the eastern half of Devon; Dumpdon and Sidbury are other examples. Other Devon hillforts are more usually either univallate (with one rampart), as in plate 27, or are of the 'south-western' type, situated on a hillslope with widely spaced ramparts (plate 25). The Iron Age hillfort at Hembury was probably abandoned some time before the end of the first millennium. Thereafter it was briefly occupied by the Roman army, who built a fort within it during their advance into Dumnonia (south-west England).

Further Reading

Hembury Fort DAS Field Guide (1988)

Berridge, P.J. 'Mesolithic Evidence from Hembury', *PDAS* 44 (1986), 163–6

Liddell, D. Interim reports on excavations at Hembury in *PDAS* 1 (1929-32), 40–63, 90–120, 162–190; *PDAS* 2 (1933–36), 133–75

Todd, M. 'Excavations at Hembury, Devon: A Summary Report', *Antiq. J.* 64 (1984), 251–68

Photograph: F.M. Griffith, Devon County Council, 26 June 1984

Plate 9

Henge between Bow and North Tawton

Like the causewayed enclosure beneath the hillfort at Hembury, this site is one whose upstanding traces have all been erased long ago. The cropmarks here represent the remains of quite a large prehistoric ceremonial structure – some 60 m by 70 m overall – which would previously have been a prominent feature of the landscape. The cropmarks show two massive banana-shaped ditches outside which the very faint traces of a paler mark survive to indicate the former presence of an outer bank on either side of the henge, made from the earth dug from the ditches. (For an explanation of how cropmarks reveal buried features, see Introduction, page 10.) This characteristic combination of inner ditch and outer bank tells us that we are not looking at a conventional defensive site but at the very distinctive features of a 'henge' – a ceremonial monument dating from the end of the Neolithic period or the very beginning of the Bronze Age. Within the henge can clearly be seen the cropmarks of an irregular ovoid of large deep pits, which may have held a setting of tall wooden posts. While a number of other henges have been certainly or tentatively identified in south-west England, this one, which was discovered by aerial reconnaissance in the drought of 1984, is the first to be positively identified as of 'Class 2' type (having two entrances) in the area. It was previously thought that this type had not been constructed further west than Dorchester in Dorset.

In the area immediately around the henge a number of smaller circular cropmarks have also been photographed. These are known as 'ring ditches' (see below, p.30) and probably represent the remains of a group of round barrows constructed in the area around the major ritual monument. The concentration of a number of different types of ceremonial and funerary monuments in a restricted area is a characteristic feature of this period, and excellent extant examples of such complexes can for example be observed on Dartmoor. In this case, however, in the heart of cultivated lowland Devon, there was no clue to the existence of this important complex until the right ground and crop conditions for cropmark production coincided with an archaeologist flying overhead. It is salutary to observe that clear though the cropmarks appear in this picture, taken in 1984, the site has barely been visible at all in subsequent summers, and nothing at all can be seen on the ground.

Further Reading

Griffith, F.M. 'Some newly discovered Ritual Monuments in mid Devon', *PPS* 51 (1985), 310–15

Harding, A.F. *Henge Monuments and Related Sites of Great Britain* (BAR Brit. Ser. 175, 1987)

Photograph: F.M. Griffith, Devon County Council, 6 July 1984

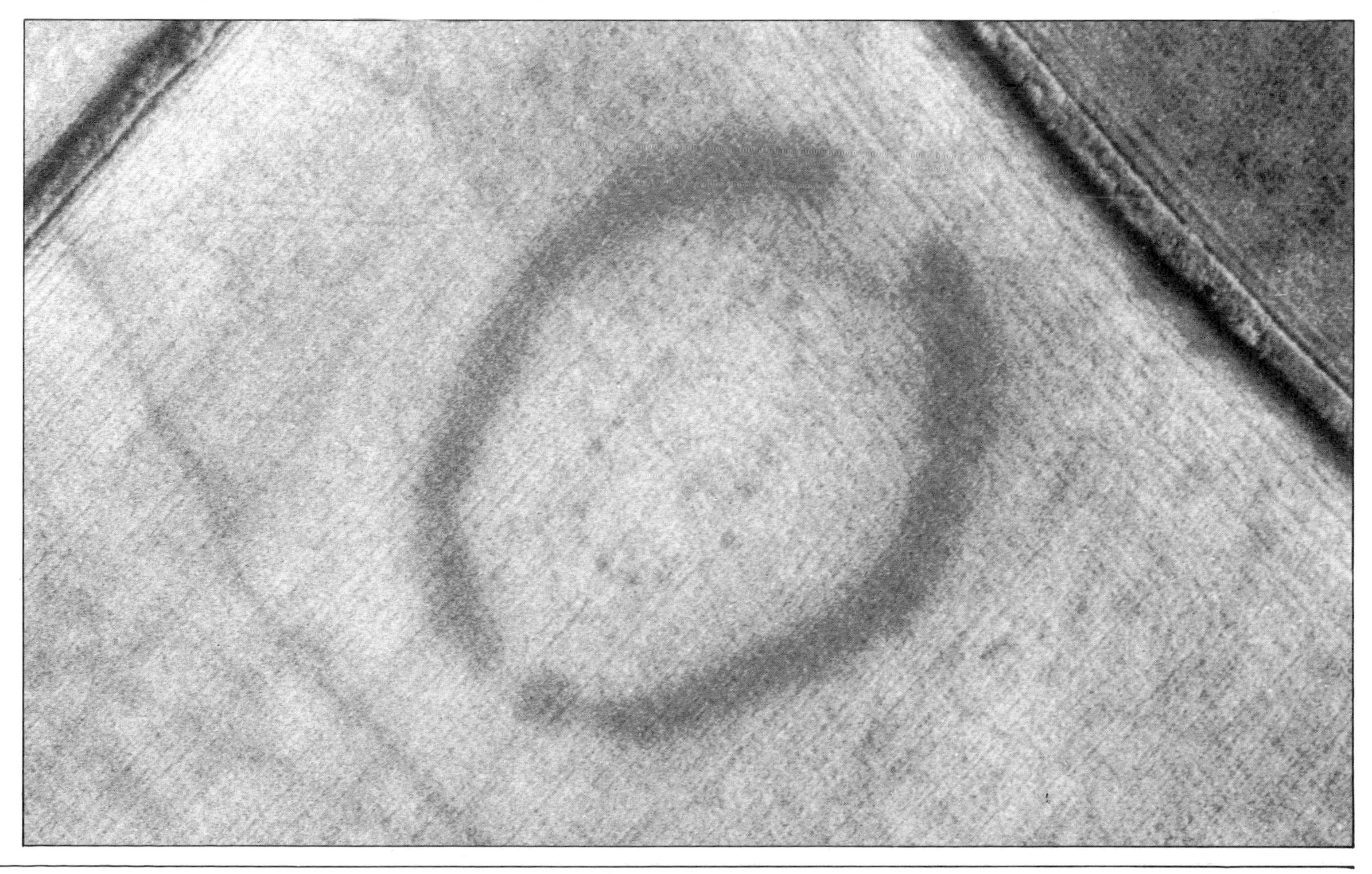

Plates 10 and 11

Ceremonial Monuments on Dartmoor

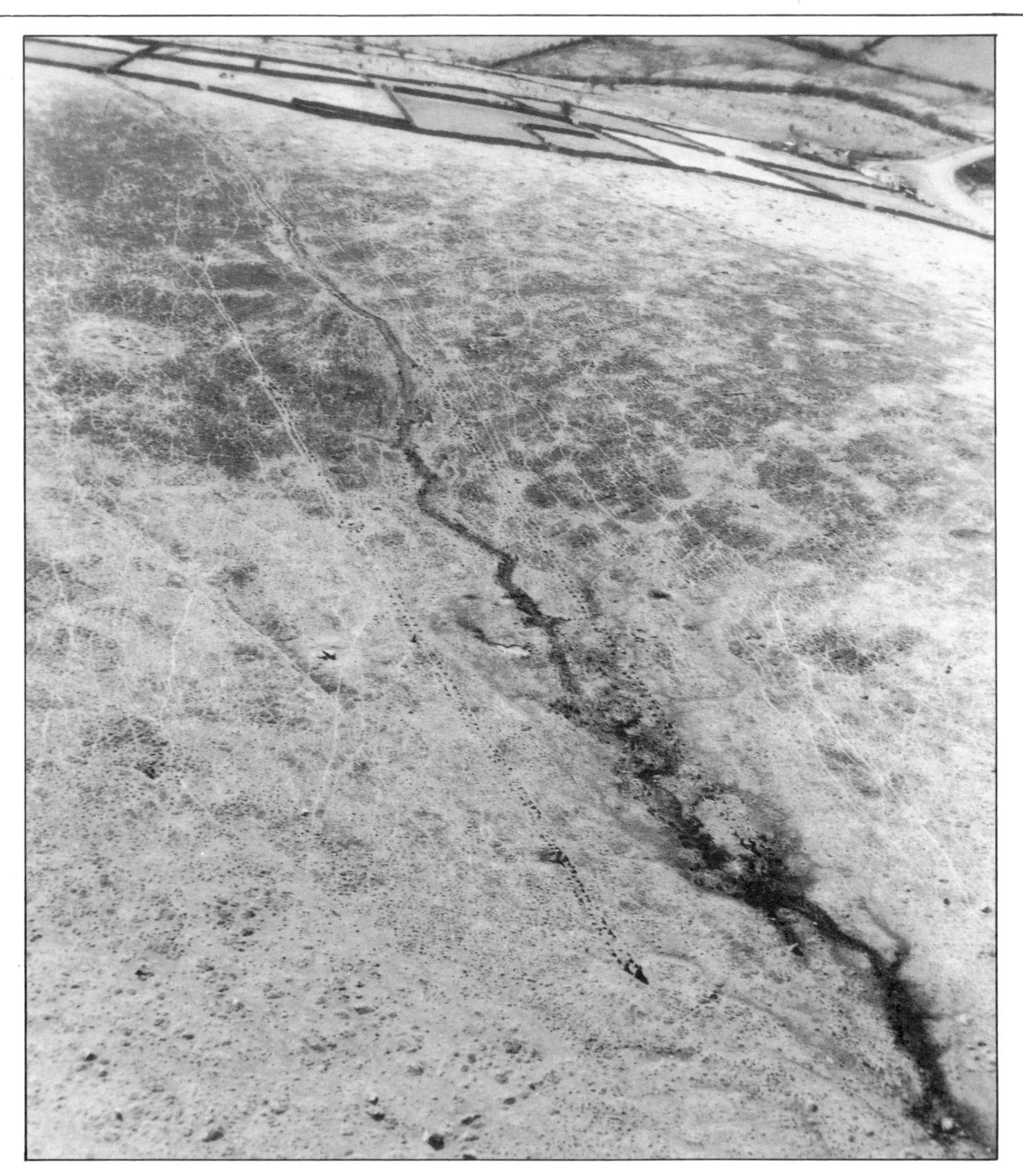

The ceremonial complex at Bow has been newly discovered; contemporary ones have long been recognized and studied on the upland areas of Dartmoor and Exmoor. There appear to be a series of foci of ritual or ceremonial activity on the moors, all dating from broadly the same time. These complexes are characterized by the presence of stone rows, stone circles, structured cairns, cists and standing stones, or by some combination of these. As in the case of the ring ditches at Bow, it is likely that not all these monuments were strictly contemporary but that once one had been constructed it attracted the builders of others to the same place. Current thinking on the subject places the main phase of this activity towards the end of the third millennium B.C., but there is a marked absence of firm dating evidence, and there is a growing suspicion among archaeologists that they may be somewhat earlier in origin. (The possibility must be borne in mind that none of the monuments visible in these complexes is necessarily the primary one: the construction of all those now visible may have focused on some now undetectable feature such as a tree, a wooden post or other ephemeral but holy object.) Well-known examples of these complexes are to be seen at Shovel Down, Glasscombe, Drizzlecombe, Merrivale and Stall Moor, but a host of other, only slightly less impressive, groups are recorded.

Plate 10 shows the two principal stone rows at Merrivale, in Walkhampton parish, from the east. Both are double rows, made up of predominantly small stones which stand approximately 0.2 – 0.7 m above ground, though they are now partially buried by peat. In most parts of Dartmoor, peat had hardly started to grow when the rows were built, so the original height of these stones would have been greater. The northern (right-hand) row is some 180 m long, and the taller stone blocking the eastern end of the row can just be made out. The southern row, on the left, is considerably longer at about 264 m. Like the northern one, a blocking stone can be seen at the eastern end, but its construction is more complex in that the row incorporates a circle of stones, representing the retaining kerb of a small cairn or barrow, about half-way along its length. This can be seen in the photograph. Further along the row a barrow lies just to the south, and from this barrow a fragmentary third, single, row runs for some distance (not visible here).

About 180 m to the south of the rows lies a stone circle, while one of the numerous barrows, cairns and cists in the vicinity can be seen in the foreground of the photograph. Merrivale, which is easily accessible from the Princetown – Tavistock road, also exhibits a particularly fine group of large hut circles of later date, as well as a mediaeval blowing house (see p.102) and relics of moorstone working. Within one of the larger hut circles an unfinished millstone made from the moorstone can be seen; R.H. Worth comments acidly that 'Col. Hamilton Smith [an earlier antiquary] had no difficulty in seeing it as a fallen cromlech'.

The second photograph shows the well-known multiple stone circle at Yellowmead, on the south-eastern side of Sheeps Tor. It should be noted that its excellent condition is due to its having been restored by the Rev. H. Breton after its excavation in 1922, but since Worth assures us that it was 'faithfully done' there seems little reason to doubt its main features. (For Worth's views on the reconstruction of Grimspound see p.37.)

The structure as it survives is a fourfold stone circle, the innermost ring of stones being close-set, the outer ones more widely spaced. Its overall diameter is about 20 m, and it is one of a group of similar monuments of which one, the multiple circle at Shovel Down, has been known for some time, but others, such as those at Glasscombe, have only recently been recognized. At present it seems that

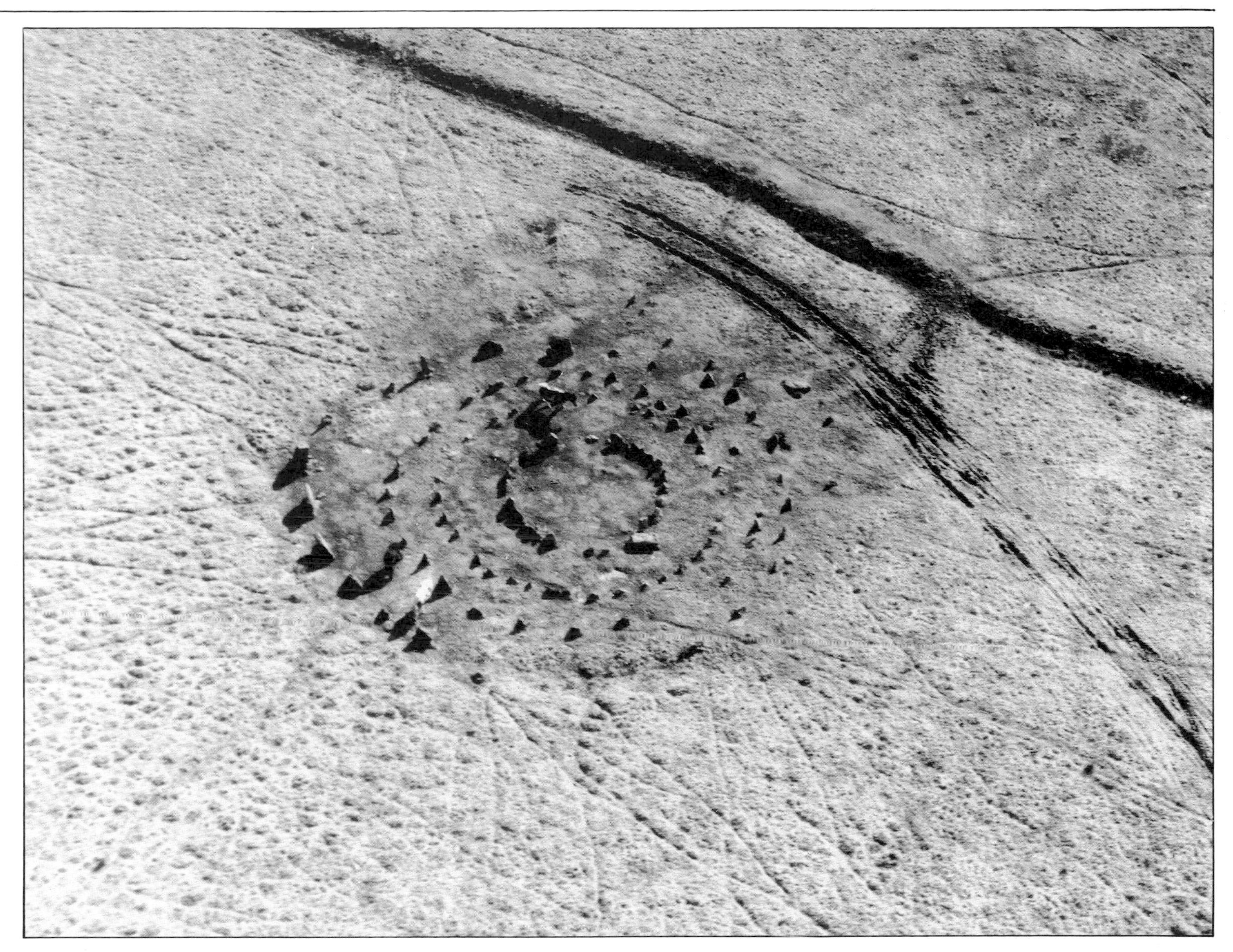

these sites should probably be viewed as related more to structured cairns than to the group of large stone circles proper; traces of a barrow mound are recorded as surviving within the innermost circle at Yellowmead. Recently further multiple circles have been identified in fieldwork by Rosemary Robinson and Judith Cosford within the mounds of existing barrows, which tends to confirm the belief that the circle at Yellowmead was originally part of the internal structure of a particularly complex structured cairn, most of whose mound has since been removed. Running out from the west side of the multiple circle at Yellowmead is a short length of what seems to be a vestigial double stone row. Again the close relationship between the circle and the row is paralleled at Shovel Down and Glasscombe, and since there are a number of other cairns in the vicinity, it seems likely that we are looking here at the remains of another 'ceremonial complex'.

Further Reading

Emmett, D.D. 'Stone Rows: the Traditional View Reconsidered', *PDAS* 37 (1979), 94–114

Grinsell, L.V. 'Dartmoor Barrows' *PDAS* 36 (1978), 85–180

Pettit, P. *Prehistoric Dartmoor* (David & Charles, 1974)

Robinson, R. & Greeves, T.A.P. 'Two Unrecorded Prehistoric Multiple Stone Rings, Glasscombe, Ugborough, South Dartmoor', *PDAS* 39 (1981), 33–6

Robinson, R. & Cosford, J. 'Dartmoor Multiple Stone Circles', *PDAS* 44 (1986), 166–70

Worth, R.H. '41st Report of the Barrow Committee', *TDA* 54 (1922), 70–3

— *Dartmoor* (David & Charles, 2nd ed. 1967)

Photographs: J.K.S. St Joseph, Cambridge University, 18 April 1967

Plate 12

Five Barrows, Exmoor

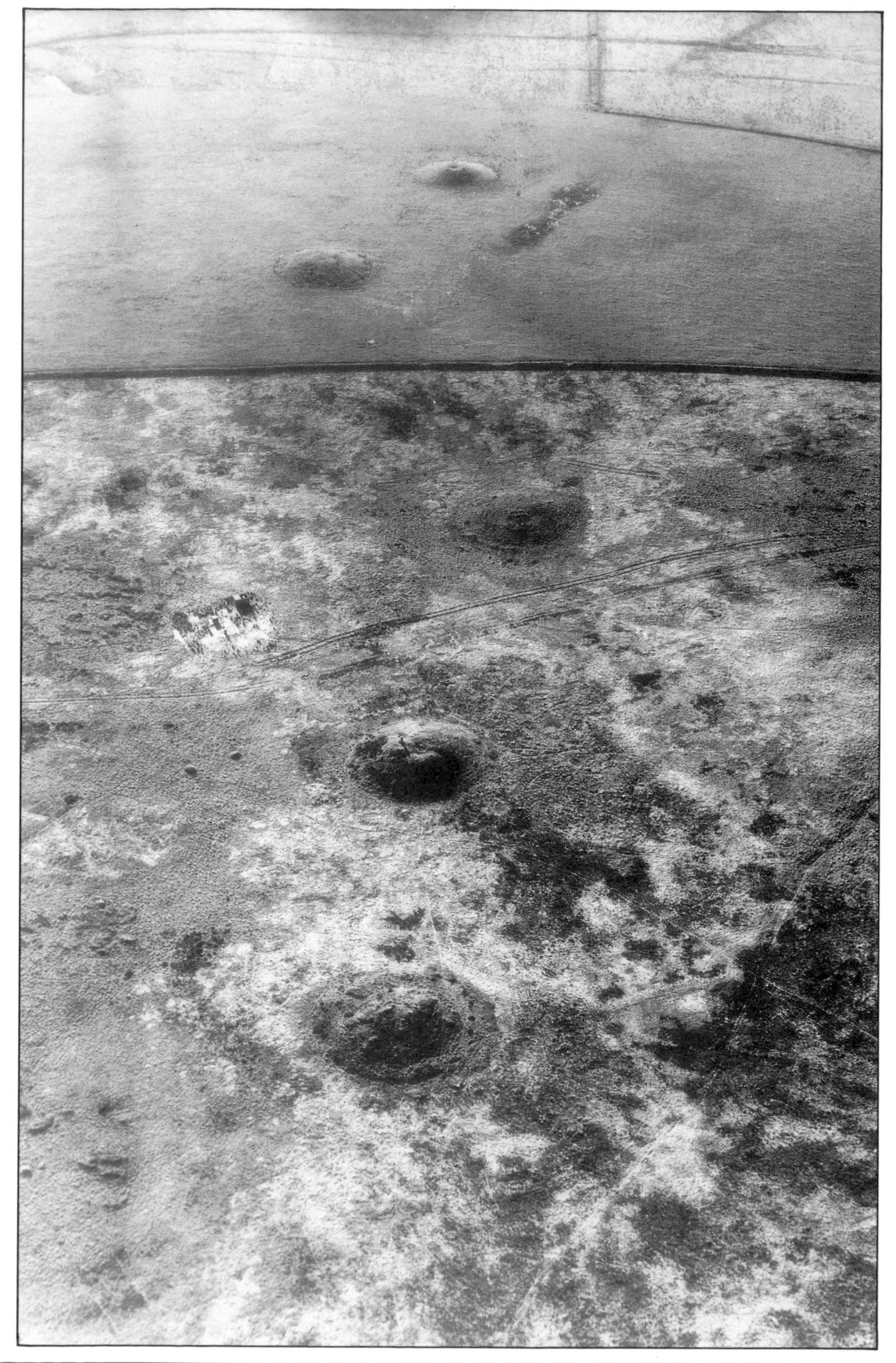

This group of round barrows on Exmoor, although known as 'Five Barrows', in fact comprises at least nine separate monuments. They occupy a crest position visible for miles around; perhaps the reason for the name is that only five stand out on the skyline. Counting both its Devon and its Somerset parts, Exmoor boasts over 300 round barrows. These include some particularly fine groups such as Five Barrows and the complex known as Chapman Barrows, a spectacular linear cemetery on the hill forming the boundary between Challacombe and Parracombe parishes. It is remarkable, in view of the wealth of Bronze Age funerary monuments on Exmoor, that settlement evidence for the period should be so elusive when compared with the extensive remains on Dartmoor. Current archaeological field survey on Exmoor is, however, locating extensive if slight prehistoric settlement remains.

Seven of the Five Barrows group exceed 25 m in diameter, and the largest is over 35 m across. This last is particularly interesting in being an example of the type known as a 'bell barrow' – one having a central mound separated from its encircling ditch by a level platform. This type of barrow is more usually associated with the chalklands of Wessex, although examples are known as far west as Cornwall. The bell barrow is often associated with grave-goods of 'Beaker' type, and might therefore be supposed to date from the very beginning of the Bronze Age. However, no member of the Five Barrows group has ever been excavated, so any suggestion as to their precise date is speculative.

Further Reading

Prehistoric Barrows on Exmoor DAS Field Guide no. 4 (1988)

Eardley-Wilmot, H. *Ancient Exmoor* (Exmoor Press, 1983)

Grinsell, L.V. *The Archaeology of Exmoor* (David & Charles, 1970)

— 'The Barrows of North Devon', *PDAS* 28 (1970), 95–129

Photograph: J.K.S. St Joseph, Cambridge University, 28 April 1966

Plate 13

Crownhill Down, South-west Dartmoor

In spite of its wealth of very fine round barrows, Dartmoor has no single group as impressive as Five Barrows on Exmoor, let alone the great prehistoric cemeteries of Wessex. The largest Devon barrow cemeteries are at Upton Pyne and Farway, in east Devon, while there are a number of smaller groups in north and west Devon. Dartmoor does not possess a comparable complex of barrows; this photograph shows one of the best groups, that at Crownhill Down on the extreme south-western edge of the moor, about 10 km north-east of Plymouth. At Crownhill Down thirteen round barrows are aligned in a classic ridge-top position, with additional outliers. The main alignment runs down the centre of the photograph, and another barrow can be seen lower left centre. The group is certainly not so spectacular as Five Barrows.

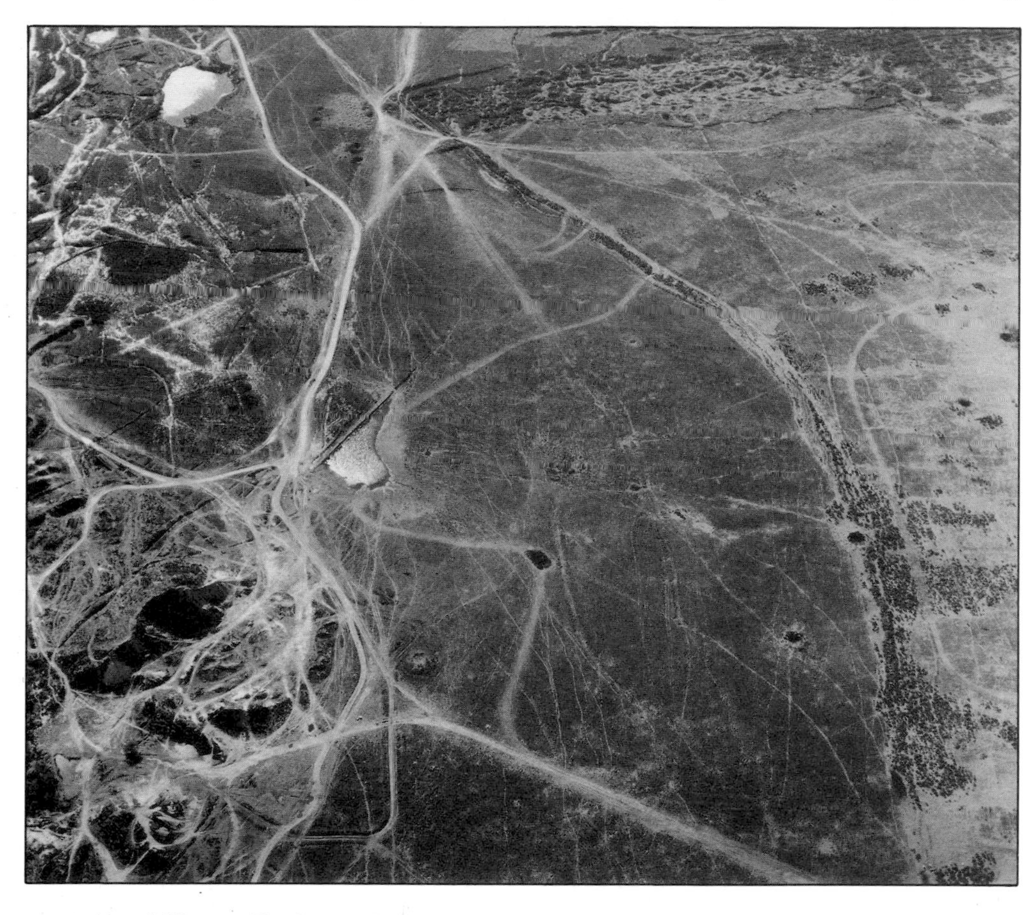

A large number of other, later, features are also to be seen here. The sharply defined linear feature passing close by the barrows and curving across the picture is a leat which provided power for the Bottle Hill Mine some 1.5 km to the south-west. Running from the centre top to the right is the end of a major area of mediaeval and later tin working which continues from the top of Crownhill Down into the valley of the Tory Brook to the west. This tinwork is particularly interesting in manifesting evidence of both streamworking and shaft mining (see p.102), including the Wheal Florence shaft, and in possessing a range of features relating to the processing of the tin. Around the top of the tinwork a number of trial pits can be seen, distinguished from the prehistoric barrows by their much sharper profiles and irregular shape. To the left of the picture the larger-scale ground disturbances are the remains of china-clay workings: immediately to the left of the photograph lies the large modern Headon China Clay Works, and the pits, reservoirs and spoilheaps here are the remains of its nineteenth-century predecessor.

To the west (right) of where this picture was taken, a remarkable range of archaeological features are preserved on the lower slopes of Crownhill Down. They include more barrows, prehistoric huts, fragments of reaves, a series of parallel linear field boundaries and medieval settlement features. These are of importance because they are typical 'Dartmoor' sites occurring on a non-granite base and at an altitude (100–200 m) where this sort of archaeological material has been entirely lost on all the other sides of the moor. In spite of its unprepossessing appearance, which is due to modern mineral-working activity and a proliferation of tracks, this area can give us a valuable insight into the past land-use of the fringe between the true upland area of Dartmoor and the surrounding lowlands.

Further Reading

Collis, J. *et al* 'The prehistoric and medieval field archaeology of Crownhill Down, Dartmoor, England', *J. Field Archaeology* 2 (1984), 1–12

Edwards, C. *An Archaeological Survey of an area surrounding Hemerdon Ball* (Devon Committee for Rescue Archaeology, 1979)

Photograph: F.M. Griffith, Devon County Council, 16 February 1988

Photograph: F.M. Griffith, Devon County Council, 16 July 1984

Photograph: F.M. Griffith, Devon County Council, 5 July 1984

Plates 14–16

Ring Ditches

The two circular marks in the field in the first photograph are 'ring ditches'. Within them the darker growth of the crop suggests a greater depth of soil than in the surrounding area: this represents the remains of the mound of a round barrow of probable early second millennium B.C. date. Both these monuments were first identified as barrows by Professor Thurstan Shaw (as a schoolboy) in the 1930s, when they were still substantial mounds, albeit spread by ploughing. They are now much flatter, though still just perceptible to the observer on the ground.

The ring around the barrow itself is the cropmark of the ditch which sometimes surrounds lowland barrows, providing the material for the mound. Where a barrow's above-ground remains have been entirely removed by cultivation, it is only by the identification of its ditch that the past existence of the barrow can be recognized. Ring ditches have long been known in other parts of Britain but were believed to be rare here until one was excavated (plate 16) in salvage conditions on the line of the A30 by the Roads Committee of Devon Archaeological Society in 1974. Since then, aerial reconnaissance has greatly increased the number of ring ditches known, and this in turn has altered our perception of the distribution of round barrows and related monuments in the heavily cultivated lowland areas.

The second photograph shows a single ring ditch which could have been destroyed unknown. The road passing the lower left-hand corner of the picture is the newly constructed North Devon Link Road, near Tiverton, and the area of disturbance near the bottom of the picture is the site of the contractors' compound for the project. Several archaeologists, including the writer, visited the road engineers at the compound in the course of the archaeological 'watching brief' during construction of the road, but the existence of the ring ditch was unknown. Although this ring ditch was unharmed by the roadworks, one cannot help wondering whether it was once part of a group. Prior identification of features before a construction project begins is the best way to ensure the opportunity for proper archaeological recording; this is an important object of the present reconnaissance project.

We know from excavation that many Bronze Age barrows had no ditch; unless they possessed deep pits or other features cutting the subsoil, all trace of these will be irretrievably lost when their mounds have been destroyed. Thus, even given that adequate resources are available for reconnaissance, the aerial archaeologist can only ever partially reconstruct the lost landscape of ceremonial monuments of this type.

Further Reading

Fox, A. 'The Upton Pyne Cemetery', *PDAS* 27 (1969), 75–8

Grinsell, L.V. 'The Barrows of South and East Devon', *PDAS* 41 (1983), 5–46

Jarvis, K. 'The Excavation of a Ring Ditch at Markham Lane, Exminster', *PDAS* 34 (1976), 62–7

Photograph: Devon Archaeological Society Roads Committee, 1974

Plate 17

Reaves, Rippon Tor, Dartmoor

One of the major advances in landscape archaeology in Britain in the last fifteen years has been the widespread recognition of large-scale systems of land division dating in broad terms from the second millennium B.C. Dartmoor was one of the first areas where such a phenomenon was observed, and locally the boundaries of these divisions are known as reaves. Their existence in many parts of Dartmoor had long been known, and they were discussed by a number of the nineteenth-century Dartmoor writers, but until a piece of detailed work in the 1960s by Elizabeth Gawne and John Somers Cocks they had generally been believed to be of mediaeval date. However, closer observation showed that the reaves – the low banks of stone and earth running across this photograph – had been built either earlier than, or at the same time as, known prehistoric features, demonstrating conclusively their prehistoric origin. Reaves often run for miles across the moor in parallel formation, as here; these are known as 'parallel reave systems', and they may cross the land with little apparent regard for the terrain. Thus the Dartmeet system, one of the largest, starts on Holne Moor and heads north, plunging right down into the Dart valley and up the other side, the reaves retaining the same alignment although not visible in the bottom of the valley. This feature of the Dartmeet reave system was one of the points observed by Gawne and Somers Cocks in their seminal paper.

Since their identification, the reave systems on Dartmoor have been the subject of intensive study, in particular by Andrew Fleming and others from Sheffield University. A programme of survey and excavation – the Dartmoor Reaves Project – extending over more than ten years has produced results of great importance. The division of the land on such a large scale (the largest reave system covers upwards of 3500 hectares) appears to indicate a high degree of social organization in the society that constructed them, and Fleming's excavations have shown that some at least of the stone banks we now see had predecessors in the form of wooden fences and the lynchets of arable fields. The main reave-building phase has been provisionally dated c. 1600–1500 B.C. The picture which is emerging of a large population living in mixed farming settlements in a highly organized society has transformed our view of Middle Bronze Age settlement on Dartmoor and elsewhere. Further analysis and excavation of the field remains will amplify the story in the future.

This photograph was taken on false-colour infra-red film, which is more sensitive to the near infra-red end of the spectrum than normal films and has its emulsions processed so as to show infra-red parts of the spectrum as red. This type of film is used in aerial work particularly by natural scientists but it is also of value to archaeologists. In this photograph its infra-red sensitive properties are used to show the differences between the 'natural' moorland vegetation (which is in fact growing on soils whose structure and productivity have been radically altered by human exploitation in the past) and the vegetation of the 'improved' grazing of the modern fields. The improved vegetation, having a greater leaf area and stronger growth, exhibits greater infra-red reflectance and shows as deep red in the picture, while the former, with a higher proportion of dead vegetation, shows as paler brown. Vegetation patterns induced by differential land-use can be very long-lived: in some cases 'improved' plots created in the prehistoric period can still be detected by infra-red photography, their better vegetation having been maintained by preferential grazing by stock. Palaeo-environmental work on the soils of such fields has confirmed that variation in the prehistoric use of the land can still be detected today.

Further Reading

Fleming, A. 'The Prehistoric Landscape of Dartmoor: part 1, South Dartmoor', *PPS* 44 (1978), 97–124

— 'The Dartmoor Reaves: Boundary Patterns and Behaviour Patterns in the Second Millennium b.c.', *PDAS* 37 (1979), 115–31

— 'The Prehistoric Landscape of Dartmoor: part 2, North and East Dartmoor', *PPS* 49 (1983), 195–242

— 'Dartmoor Reaves', *Devon Archaeol.* 3 (1985), 1–6

Gawne, E. and Somers Cocks, J. 'Parallel Reaves on Dartmoor', *TDA* 100 (1968), 277–91

Photograph: National Monuments Record, RCHME, 21 April 1980

Plate 18

Reaves, Easdon Down, Dartmoor

Easdon Down lies in North Bovey parish, isolated from the principal unenclosed areas of Dartmoor. The hill itself is now an island of 'unimproved' land surrounded by more recent fields. The photograph shows that the open area of the hill (upper left), under rough grazing, still preserves a pattern of prehistoric reaves very much like that in the last photograph and the whole is overlain by later ridge-and-furrow cultivation.

The reaves surviving in the landscape have conditioned the layout of more recent fields, which follow the lines of the reaves themselves. The presence of the unchanged parallel reave system on the open ground enables the archaeologist to trace its course into the enclosed land with a fair degree of confidence.

Further Reading

See p.33.

Photograph: National Monuments Record, RCHME, 18 May 1977

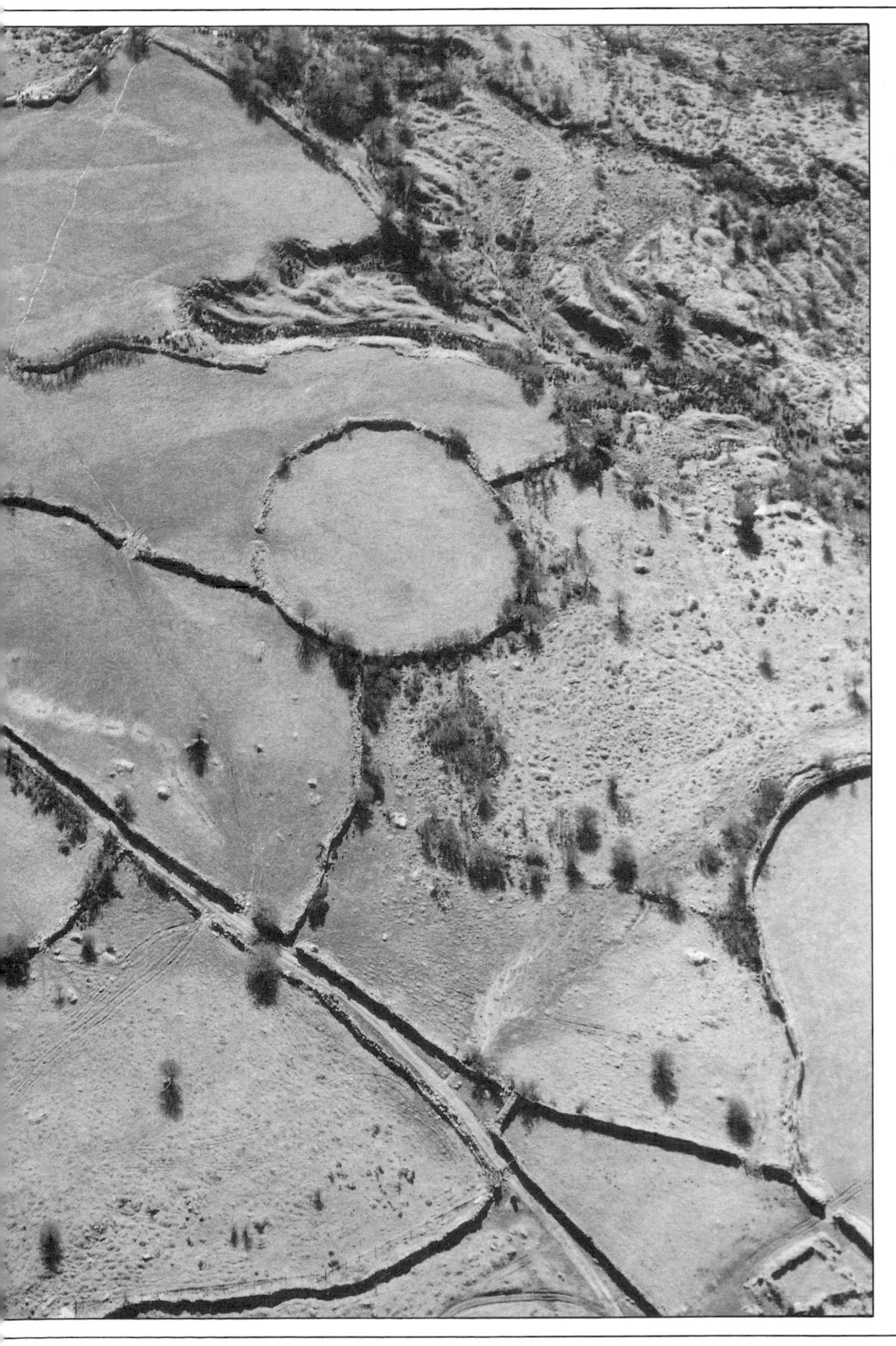

Plate 19

Prehistoric Enclosures, Walkhampton

This photograph shows an example of a phenomenon similar to the last. At Routrundle we see two prehistoric enclosures like those in many parts of Dartmoor on the open moor, one with a single hut circle surviving within it. They now form part of a continuous field system which can be seen to be later in date than the two enclosures.

The place-name 'Routrundle' itself probably reflects the existence of the features here. One element of the name contains the Old English word 'trendel' or 'tryndel', which means a circle or ring. In this case the circle in question could be either one of the round enclosures or the hut circle within. We find the same word in the name of 'The Trendle', a hilltop earthwork enclosure near Tavistock.

In the extreme bottom left of the photograph the line of the old railway from Yelverton to Princetown can be seen. This was part of the Dartmoor Railway which was built circa 1819–24 with the objects of carrying granite down from the moorland quarries and of carrying manure and lime to the moorland farms and coal and supplies to the village of Princetown and the prison.

Further Reading

Worth, R.H. *Dartmoor* (David & Charles, 2nd ed. 1967) pp. 152–3

Photograph: F.M. Griffith, Devon County Council, 16 February 1988

Plate 20

Riders Rings, South Brent, Dartmoor

The complex prehistoric enclosure known as Riders Rings is situated on the brow of the western side of the steep valley of the River Avon. It is a large and striking settlement. The southern enclosure (to the left of the picture), covering some 1.32 hectares and containing at least fifteen round houses, appears to be the primary one to which the northern enclosure was subsequently added. Around the inside edge of the northern enclosure, and in some places in the southern one, a series of small enclosed 'courts' can be seen; it has been suggested that these are garden plots or animal pounds. If the latter, they would reinforce the interpretation of this settlement as that of a pastoral community, which its position certainly suggests.

Riders Rings is one of the most handsome and well-constructed of the prehistoric Dartmoor 'pounds'. In some places the stone facing on the outer and inner walls can still be seen. On the opposite side of the valley, on Smallbrook Plains and Dockwell Ridge, there are numerous other examples of enclosed groups of hut circles to be seen, and to the south of the Rings are yet more enclosures and many unenclosed huts as well. The whole of the Avon valley seems to have been intensively exploited in the earlier part of the second millennium B.C. but this is a rather different settlement pattern from that shown, for example, on Rippon Tor (plate 17). In the immediate vicinity of Riders Rings there are neither reaves nor visible remains of field systems, though this cannot be taken to mean that no cultivation was taking place.

Running around the side of the hill above and through the enclosures are several later leats. These served to drive water-wheels at clayworkings to the south of Riders Rings.

Further Reading

Worth, R.H. 'Dartmoor Exploration Committee, Twelfth Report', *TDA* 67 (1935), 115–19

Photograph: F.M. Griffith, Devon County Council, 17 March 1987

Plate 21

Grimspound, Manaton, Dartmoor

One of the most well-known and often visited of all the archaeological sites on Dartmoor, Grimspound appears to differ from most of the other enclosed settlements on the moor only in the unusually massive construction of its walls. This may well result more from the ready availability of building materials than any exceptional defensive need, for the 'pound' is situated in a saddle between two hills rather than in an optimum position for defence.

Some of the hut circles within the enclosure were excavated in 1894–5 as the very first project of the Devonshire Association's Dartmoor Exploration Committee, whose members included among others the Rev. Sabine Baring-Gould. Although no pottery was found, flint and stone artefacts were recovered from the floors of the round houses. In spite of the absence of pottery reported by the excavators, Grimspound appears to belong in the same general date-range as other enclosed Dartmoor settlements, perhaps having its origin in the earlier second millennium B.C. (though see also p.39). While the round houses were excavated with rather less precision than would be the case nowadays (the report mentions 'completely exploring' two in one day!) care was taken not to remove earthfast stones and the huts were subsequently reconstructed. (The reconstruction of the site was not to everyone's taste, however. The somewhat monumental appearance of the rebuilt entrance in the south-east of the enclosure has often been criticized, while of the walls R.H. Worth, in *Dartmoor* pp. 142–3, commented: 'I have always held it was a mistake to rebuild the structure in accordance with the Committee's views of what it ought to be ... And so I ventured to dissent from the conclusions of my colleagues: a task a little difficult for the youngest member.')

Since the photograph was taken in 1966, this monument has been subjected to a considerable amount of erosion through the sheer number of visitors it receives each year. A modern photograph would show significantly more bare areas where vegetation has been worn away by the feet of walkers; this is an increasing problem on the more popular and accessible archaeological sites throughout Britain.

Further Reading

Baring Gould, S. *et al* 'First Report of the Dartmoor Exploration Committee: The Exploration of Grimspound', *TDA* 26 (1894), 101–21

Worth, R.H. *Dartmoor* (David & Charles, 2nd ed. 1967), 142–4, 150–53

Photograph: J.K.S. St Joseph, Cambridge University, 28 April 1966

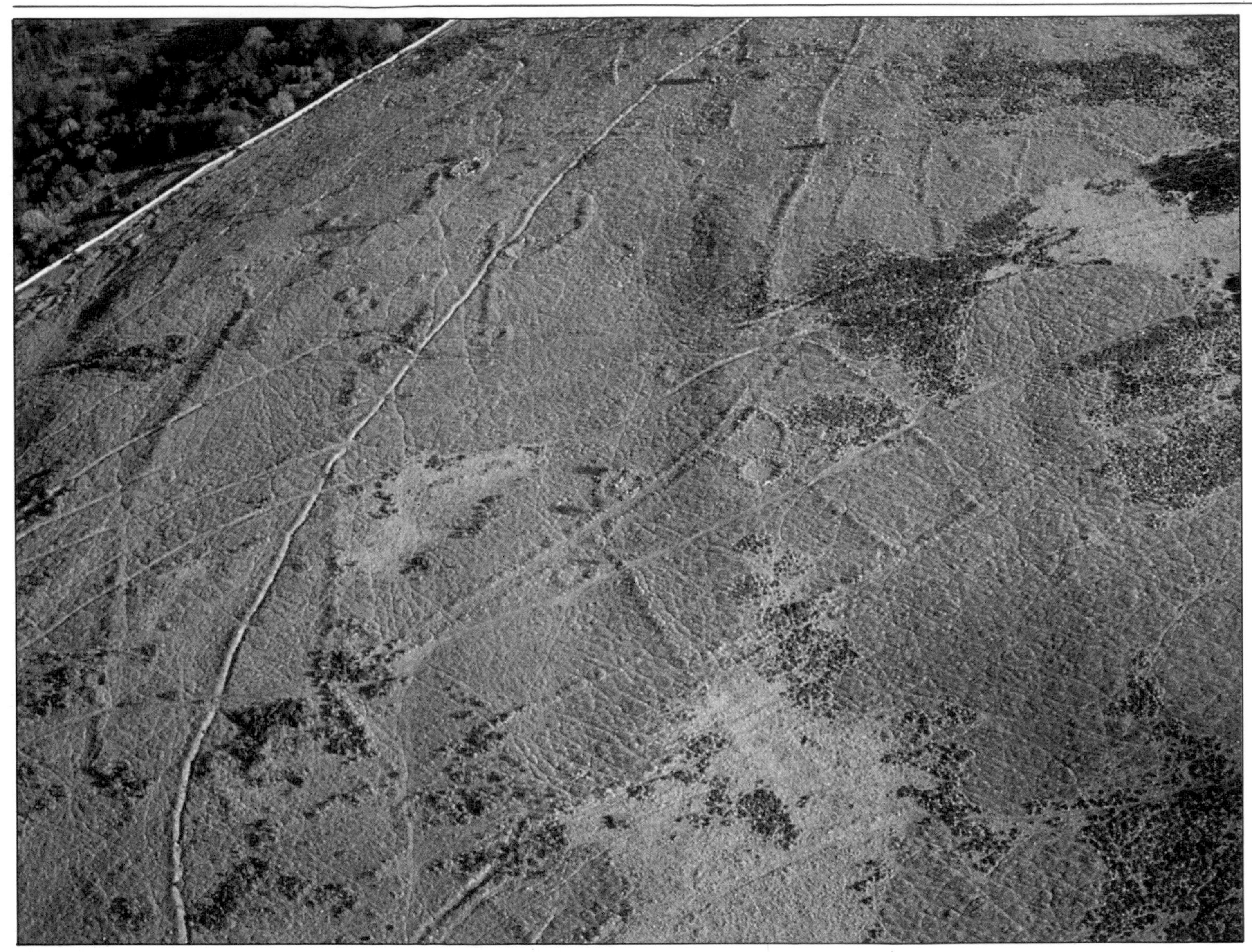

Plate 22

Throwleigh Common, Dartmoor

Not all settlement on Dartmoor is in compact enclosures such as those shown in the previous two photographs. Here on Throwleigh Common, on the north side of the moor, the round houses and fields are laid out in a more complicated pattern. The vegetation of the moor is also denser and more difficult in this area, and the archaeologist on the ground may have some trouble in disentangling the archaeological remains amidst the bracken (the light brown vegetation) and the gorse (dark green). This is an instance where an air photograph of upstanding features can be very helpful in the process of making sense of a complicated archaeological landscape. The features show particularly clearly in this picture, which was taken in April when the vegetation was at its lowest, and in the late afternoon so that the low sunlight made the slight features stand out in sharp relief.

The photograph shows a series of small hut circles or round houses scattered about in a rather irregular pattern of small fields and enclosures. A droveway, defined by two banks, runs through the settlement, and from its apparent relationship to other visible features we can start to build up a tentative framework for the chronological development of the settlement.

Further Reading

Fleming, A. 'The Prehistoric Landscape of Dartmoor, Part 2: North and East Dartmoor', *PPS* 49 (1983), 195–241

Fox, A. 'Celtic Fields and Farms on Dartmoor', *PPS* 20 (1954), 87–102

Price, D. G. 'Site and Settlement on Throwleigh Common', *TDA* 118 (1986), 85–92

Photograph: F.M. Griffith, 15 April 1984

Plate 23

Settlement Enclosure at Shaugh Moor, South Dartmoor

This is the lowest altitude photograph in this book. Taken not from an aircraft but from a crane, it shows the excavation of a complete Dartmoor enclosure – the only one that has ever been fully excavated. The enclosure lies in the midst of the china-clay workings on Shaugh Moor and had for many years been left intact, although surrounded by waste heaps and even flooded for a while with slurry from the workings. The enclosure was excavated as part of a major archaeological rescue project carried out on south-west Dartmoor in the late 1970s. This was undertaken in advance of a new phase of the dumping of waste from china-clay workings which was to bury a complex archaeological landscape, including the site seen here. The project, which was executed by DoE's Central Excavation Unit with the co-operation of the china-clay company concerned, involved extensive field survey and the excavation of parts of reaves and a series of cairns. This enclosure was the largest single site to be excavated.

The enclosure wall proved to have two main phases of construction, dating from the fourteenth and thirteenth centuries B.C. Occupation of the site had however started well before the wall was built, and the excavator suggested that the total life of the settlement could have been as long as from circa 1650 B.C. to 700 B.C., though it was not necessarily occupied continuously. Underneath the stone round houses that can be seen here, remains of their timber predecessors were found. A similar succession from timber to stone houses has been found in excavations elsewhere on Dartmoor and it is now clear that there were many timber houses of which no trace survives. It is therefore not reasonable to make population estimates from the number and distribution only of stone hut circles on the moor, as has been attempted (with some disregard for the long period during which such houses were current) in the past.

The houses in the enclosure had no hearths; this led to the suggestion that they may have been occupied only seasonally in the summer, perhaps by transhumant herdspeople. The enclosure had no entrance, and no evidence for the presence of animals within it was found. It may therefore have been built to keep them out of rather than in the enclosure.

The fact that this settlement started as an open site, only enclosed part way through its life, should remind us that, informative as the discovery of lowland enclosed sites in the form of cropmarks may be, it can reveal to us only one part of the total potential range of settlement types that formerly existed in the landscape. The identification of unenclosed settlement sites requires other strategies and techniques.

Further Reading

Smith, K. 'The Excavation of a Bronze Age Enclosure on Shaugh Moor', *Devon Archaeol.* 3 (1985), 6–13

Wainwright, G.J. and Smith, K. 'The Shaugh Moor Project: Second Report – The Enclosure', *PPS* 46 (1980), 65–122

Photograph: Central Excavation Unit, Department of the Environment, 1978

Plate 24

Shoulsbarrow Hillfort, Exmoor

The hillfort has traditionally been believed to be a characteristic settlement feature of the Iron Age (the later first millennium B.C.), but evidence from excavations in other parts of the country now indicates that the origins of at least some hillforts date back well into the second millennium. We know that some neolithic societies also adopted hillfort-like defensive settlements, as at Hembury (above, p.24) and at Carn Brea in Cornwall, and it is becoming increasingly clear that defended sites of hillfort type are far from peculiar to the Iron Age. Excavations on hillforts in Devon have in general been very limited in extent and not conspicuously successful in finding good dating evidence, so the origins and date of most such sites in this county remain rather uncertain. The results of the total excavation of the Shaugh Moor enclosure (above), which demonstrated that occupation of the site pre-dated the construction of the enclosure wall, should remind us of the possibility that partial excavation, particularly of a hillfort's defences, may provide a very misleading impression of the true date of the 'foundation' of a particular settlement.

This photograph shows Shoulsbarrow, or Shoulsbury, which lies on the southern side of Exmoor. Though always described as a hillfort, the site is somewhat enigmatic: its plan is squarer than the majority of known hillforts, and it is often suggested that the construction of the site was unfinished, since the western (right-hand) outer rampart does not extend right up to the edge of the steeper slope (away from the camera) as would usually be expected. Shoulsbarrow certainly exhibits a classic hillfort siting, its views extending from South Wales to Bodmin Moor, but its position is so bleak that it has been doubted whether it was permanently occupied. We have already encountered the suggestion that the Shaugh Moor enclosure was a seasonal site, and it is possible that in the future more evidence for seasonality in prehistoric settlement will be recognized.

Further Reading

Grinsell, L.V. *Ancient Exmoor* (David & Charles, 1970)

Whybrow, C. 'Some Multivallate Hill-forts on Exmoor and in North Devon', *PDAS* 25 (1967), 1–18

Photograph: J.K.S. St Joseph, Cambridge University, 27 June 1953 (Crown copyright)

Plates 25 and 26

Milber Down Hillfort, near Newton Abbot

Milber Down, like Clovelly Dykes (front cover) is a typical 'south-western' hillfort. This type was first defined by Lady (Aileen) Fox in 1952 and is characterized by widely spaced ramparts which, she suggested, were to provide additional space for the protection of flocks and herds. The inference was drawn that these hillforts therefore related to a predominantly pastoral society. It is clear that this Iron Age hillfort did not fulfil the same role as, for example, Hembury, east Devon (page 24): it is sited on gently rising ground rather than a steep spur, and its ramparts can never have been so formidable. Excavations in 1937–8 produced evidence for the late Iron Age occupation of the hillfort itself, and of a small Roman site – either a farm or a small military post – known as 'Milber Little Camp' to the south-east.

The two photographs show how the site has changed between 1952 and 1984. Scrub has grown up over part of the site and one quarter of the defences has been lost: the rampart is now visible only as a cropmark. The 'Little Camp' has been almost obliterated by the construction of an abattoir (bottom centre). Observation of the site in dry conditions has on two occasions (1979, Sean Goddard; 1984, the writer) revealed the presence of a D-shaped enclosure (centre right) not previously known. The relationship of this enclosure to the hillfort is unknown, but its discovery demonstrates the fact that it is necessary for the aerial observer to keep an eye even on well-known and often-photographed sites: new information may frequently be forthcoming.

Further Reading

Milber Down DAS Field Guide no. 1 (1987)

Fox, A. 'Hillslope forts and related earthworks in South-West England and South Wales', *Archaeol. J.* 109 (1952), 1–22

Fox, A., Radford, C.A.R. and Shorter, A.H. 'Report on Excavations at Milber Down, 1937–8', *PDAS* 4 (1949–50), 27–65

Photograph: J.K.S. St Joseph, Cambridge University, 23 June 1952 (Crown copyright)
Photograph: F.M. Griffith, Devon County Council, 11 July 1984

Plate 27

Hillfort, Stoke Rivers

This hillfort, known as Stoke or Beara Castle, is a univallate enclosure sited on the top of a gentle rise. Although usually called a hillfort, the term is perhaps a little grand for this defensive enclosure, which is typical of a number of north Devon sites of probable first millennium date. Indeed, this site lies within sight of three others of the same sort: those at Mockham Down, Smythapark and Shoulsbarrow (for the last see p.40). Observations made when a pipe-trench was cut through the site demonstrated the presence of a berm about one metre wide between the rampart and the ditch; no trace of this can be seen on the surface.

What is interesting about this particular photograph is that, although the hedge that once outlined the whole circuit of the rampart has in large part been removed, the line of the rampart is still visible as an earthwork. Comparison of this photograph with that of the site in north-west Devon shown in the Introduction (p.8) will give an insight into the way in which a monument can be gradually eroded but can still be visible in the right conditions. Where the road crosses the rampart it may be seen to rise up slightly: this is particularly evident on a visit to the site. On a country road such as this, where the construction of the road probably did not involve deep earth-moving, the road simply rides over the top of the bank. The archaeological surveyor will watch out for a feature of this sort when examining a potential prehistoric site. This, or the presence of a short length of curving hedge, such as those shown here and in the next photograph, can often be the first clue to the existence of an enclosure.

Further Reading

Grinsell, L.V. *The Archaeology of Exmoor* (David & Charles, 1970)

Fox, A. '27th Report on Archaeology and Early History', *TDA* 95 (1963), 81–2

Photograph: F.M. Griffith, Devon County Council, 30 January 1987

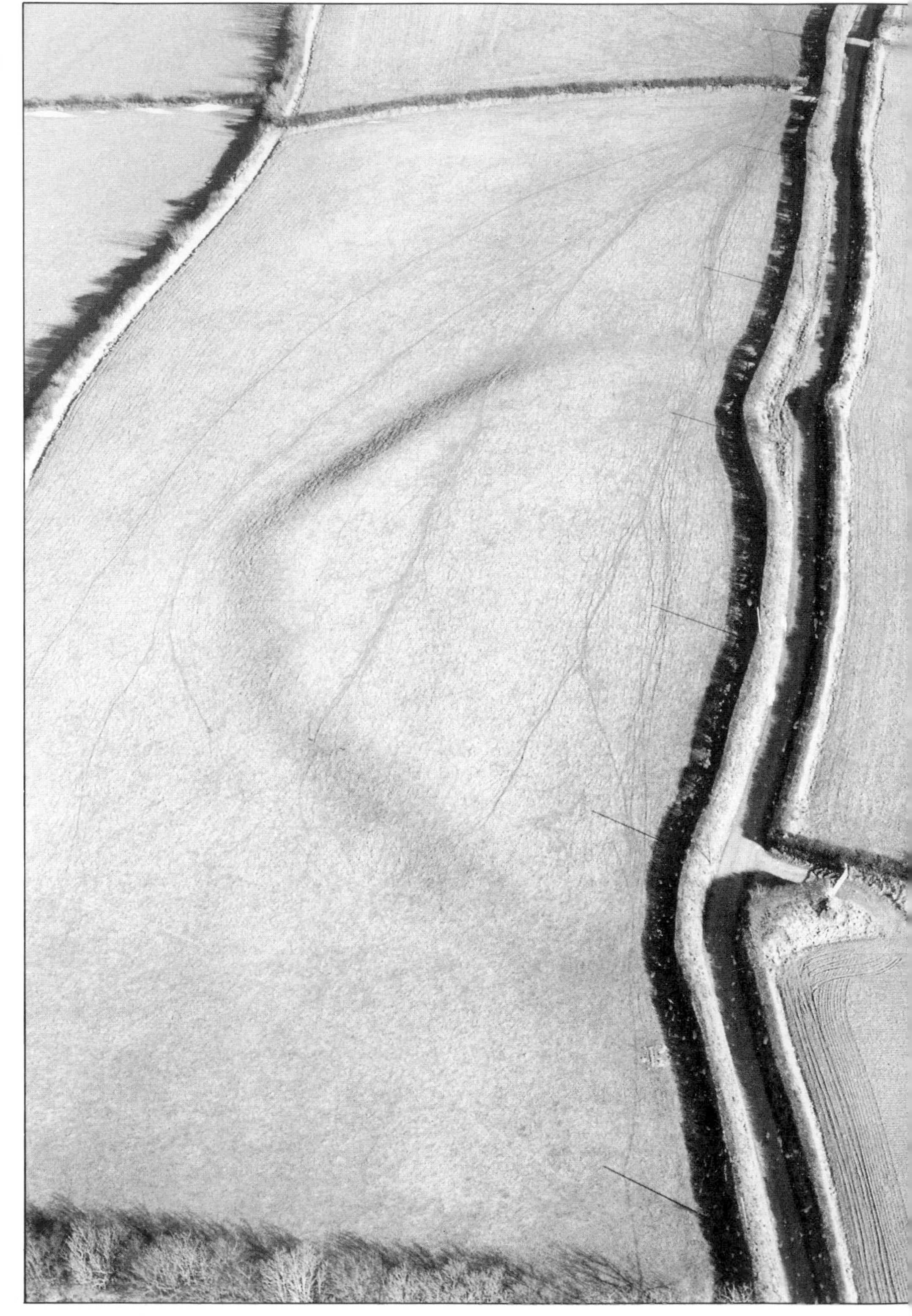

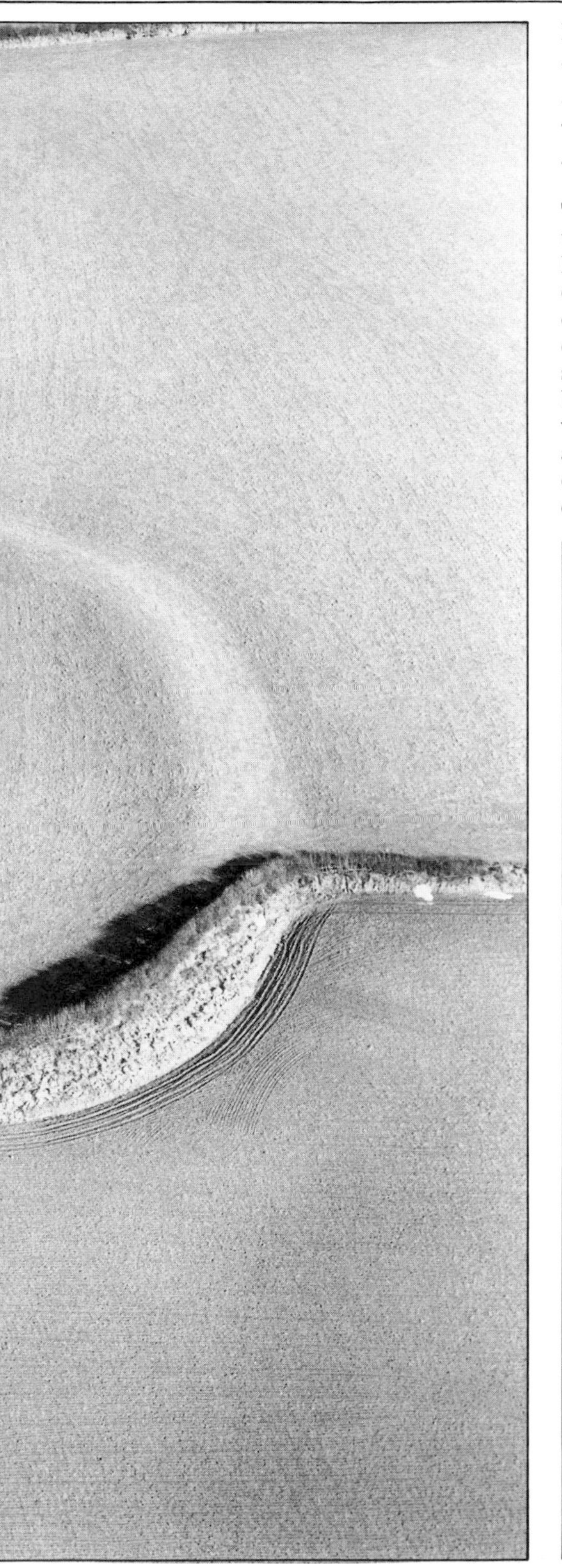

Plate 28

Enclosure near Bideford

This small hilltop enclosure is a stage further eroded than that at Stoke Rivers (opposite). The curving hedge on its lower side represents the line of the original bank, and the cropmark of the enclosure ditch can clearly be seen to be running outside it. The ditch continues all the way round the site and still survives below the hedgebank, but all trace of the bank has been lost within the area of the field. Even without the cropmark it should have been possible for an acute observer to identify the existence of this enclosure from the evidence of the curving hedge and ditch.

The cam-like shape of this enclosure is quite unusual in Devon. The location of the entrance through the bank and ditch is not entirely clear, but it is probably in the mouth of the projecting part. Very often a detail like this will become clear only when photographs taken on different occasions are compared; so far this site has been recorded only once. Especially for more complex sites, photography spread over a number of years and in varying crop conditions is essential for reliable photo-interpretation.

Further Reading

Griffith, F.M. 'Aerial Reconnaissance in Devon in 1984: A Preliminary Report and the Discovery of a Hillfort', *PDAS* 42 (1984), 7–10 (for the discovery of a similar site)

Photograph: F.M. Griffith, Devon County Council, 28 June 1984

Plate 29

Embury Beacon, Hartland

Some inland hillforts such as Hembury in east Devon (plate 8) are built in naturally strongly defended situations. Other first millennium B.C. settlements made use of defensible coastal locations: Embury Beacon, on the Hartland coast of north-west Devon, and Bolt Tail, in Malborough parish on the south Devon coast, are examples of this type. They are known as 'promontory forts' since they occupy a piece of land projecting into the sea; such sites are particularly to be found on the north Cornish and Welsh coasts.

Unfortunately, Embury, constructed on cliffs of the slates and shales of the Hartland peninsula (see plate 2) has been hard hit by coastal erosion over the years, and all that can now be seen are the outer (inland) rampart, with a complex entrance, and a short section of the inner (seaward) rampart. It has been estimated that three-quarters of the original area of the site has been lost, and this includes virtually all the actual occupation area within the inner rampart.

In 1972–3 limited excavations were carried out to try to rescue some information from the interior of the site before its disappearance, and this demonstrated the presence of post-built structures within the inner rampart as well as traces of a gateway. The excavator, who worked on the site throughout the winter, observed that the buildings must have been very well constructed to survive in such an exposed spot! The need for defence must certainly have been perceived as very strong for people to have occupied a site such as this, or that of The Rumps cliff-castle in Cornwall.

Further Reading

Jefferies, J.S. 'An Excavation at the Coastal Promontory Fort of Embury Beacon, Devon', *PPS* 40 (1974), 136–56

Photograph: F.M. Griffith, Devon County Council, 22 December 1986

Plate 30

Field System, East Ogwell

In the hinterland of Tor Bay the landscape contains frequent outcrops of Devonian limestone among the later Permian rocks; these are a general feature of the scenery of the area around the Teign and the Dart (see also, for example plate 3). Although the soils overlying the limestone bedrock are very variable, the limestone in some places has only a very thin cover of poor soil (of the Torbryan series).

The identification of archaeological sites on the limestone requires different techniques from those used in other parts of lowland Devon. Cropmarks indicative of ditched features will be virtually non-existent: people seldom dug ditches into solid limestone! However, the thin poor soils with their limited water-retaining capacities, and the friability of the underlying rock, mean that nowadays many fields on limestone are seldom or never ploughed. Paradoxically, it is the very slightness of the soil cover on sites in this area that can be a factor in their preservation as upstanding monuments.

The photograph shows an example: part of a system of small fields, identified by their dividing banks. The low lynchets of the fields, being stony, have survived quite well, and the modern field has not been vigorously ploughed. The survival of field systems of this type on the Torbay limestone was discovered relatively recently by a group of local fieldworkers who over a number of years carried out a complete survey of the area and subsequently published their findings. The dating of these sites is difficult, but a date in the later first millennium B.C. has been suggested.

Like many low earthworks, the banks of this field system are often quite hard to see, either on the ground or from the air. This photograph shows them clearly, but the writer has several times flown over this site in summer and seen barely any trace of them. The photograph was taken at midwinter, which is the optimum time for recording this particular site.

Further Reading

Gallant, L., Luxton, N. and Collman, M. 'Ancient Fields on the South Devon Limestone Plateau', *PDAS* 43 (1985), 23–38

Silvester, R.J. 'The Prehistoric Open Settlement at Dainton, South Devon', *PDAS* 38 (1980), 17–48

Photograph: F.M. Griffith, Devon County Council, 23 December 1986

Photograph: J.K.S. St Joseph, Cambridge University, 3 July 1975

Plates 31 and 32

Settlement Site at Pond Farm, Alphington

The archaeological site represented by the cropmarks on either side of the new A30 road south of Exeter was recorded from the air by Professor St Joseph (left-hand photograph) as the road was being built. Archaeologists of the Devon Archaeological Society's Roads Committee, undertaking rescue work during construction of the road in 1974–5, became aware of the site's existence from air photographs only when work on the road had actually started. A limited rescue excavation was then undertaken. It is interesting to note that even such apparently substantial elements as the ditch of the enclosure had not been identified during the archaeological observation of the contractors' topsoil stripping: it is often very difficult to recognize archaeological features in these conditions.

The site was found to be that of a Romano-British farm, and a variety of enclosures, paddocks, etc. can be seen. The circular enclosure by the road cutting may be earlier in date. The excavation at the time of the road construction was limited in extent, but produced a good assemblage of pottery to help to date the site. Since then, the rest of it has been protected by scheduling as an Ancient Monument, and its condition in 1984 (right-hand photograph) remains stable.

The importance of aerial reconnaissance in identifying archaeological sites like this well in advance of a development such as road construction is obvious: both the scale and quality of the excavation and the timetable of the road contractors are best served if such a site is known at the planning stage and excavation can be programmed to take place before construction work starts.

Further Reading

Jarvis, K. 'The M5 Motorway and the Peamore–Pocombe Link', *PDAS* 34 (1976), 42–72

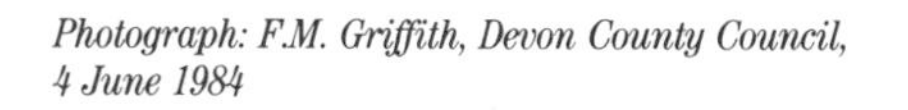

Photograph: F.M. Griffith, Devon County Council, 4 June 1984

Plate 33

Central Exeter in 1952

This photograph, taken by Professor St Joseph, shows a very different Exeter from that which we know today. There are extensive open areas where bomb-damaged buildings have been cleared in the Bedford Circus area (top centre) and west of South Street. On the other hand, the area of Quay Lane and Coombe Street (bottom right) was still a clutter of little houses, now almost all gone, and where the Guildhall Shopping Centre now stands the mediaeval pattern of narrow streets still survived at the time of this photograph. Post-war rebuilding can be seen in progress at the top of High Street.

In the Close, outside the west front of the Cathedral, St Mary Major Church may be seen. This was demolished in 1970.

Further Reading

Venning, N. *Exeter: the Blitz and Rebirth of the City* (Devon Books, 1988)

Photograph: J.K.S. St Joseph, Cambridge University, 24 June 1952 (Crown copyright)

Plate 34

Excavations in the Cathedral Close, Exeter, in 1973

Professor St Joseph photographed the Close again after the demolition of St Mary Major Church. This picture shows the excavations carried out on its site by Exeter Museums Archaeological Field Unit, in advance of the proposed construction of an underground car park on the site. The excavation demonstrated that St Mary Major occupied the site of the Anglo-Saxon minster and cathedral church which was later succeeded by the present cathedral nearby. (Parts of the fabric of the Anglo-Saxon church are thought to have survived within the mediaeval church which was pulled down in the nineteenth century to be replaced by the Victorian church seen in the picture below.)

In this photograph the excavation's other great discovery can be seen: the bath-house of the Roman Second Augustan Legion, which was stationed at Exeter in the middle of the first century A.D. It was

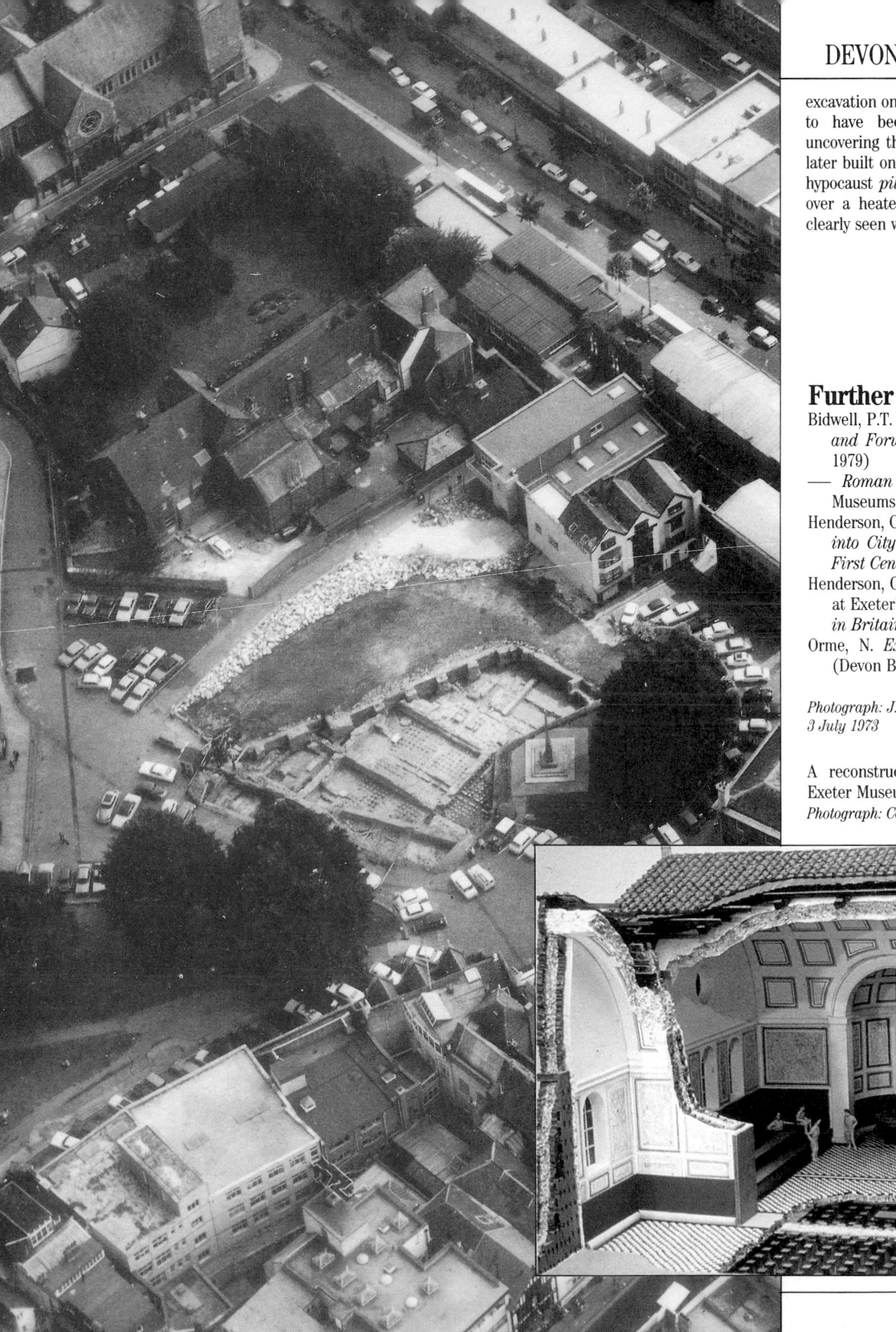

excavation on this site that conclusively proved Exeter to have been a legionary fortress, as well as uncovering the Roman forum and basilica that were later built on the site of the military bath-house. The hypocaust *pilae* (pillars of tiles supporting the floor over a heated air-space) of the bath-house can be clearly seen within the area of the excavation.

Further Reading

Bidwell, P.T. *The Legionary Bath-house and Basilica and Forum at Exeter* (Exeter Archaeol. Rep. 1, 1979)

— *Roman Exeter, Fortress and Town* (Exeter Museums, 1980)

Henderson, C.G. 'Exeter' in (ed.) Webster, G. *Fortress into City: the Consolidation of Roman Britain, First Century A.D.* (Batsford, 1988)

Henderson, C.G. and Bidwell, P.T. 'The Saxon Minster at Exeter' in (ed.) Pearce, S.M. *The Early Church in Britain and Ireland* (BAR Brit. Ser. 102, 1982)

Orme, N. *Exeter Cathedral As It Was 1050–1550* (Devon Books, 1986)

Photograph: J.K.S. St Joseph, Cambridge University, 3 July 1973

A reconstruction of the legionary bath-house, in Exeter Museum.
Photograph: Courtesy of Exeter City Museums

Plate 35

The Roman Fort at Okehampton

This fort dates from the Roman conquest of south-west England and is thus broadly contemporary with the legionary fortress at Exeter (above). It was constructed somewhere between A.D. 50 and 70 and is one of a series of forts now being identified in the region; another is shown below. Aerial photography has played an important role in the discovery of these sites – as it has over the whole Roman Empire – and in recent years the picture of Roman military activity in south-west England has been much changed.

The photograph shows the typical 'playing card' shape of a Roman fort: a rectangle with rounded corners. The two ditches around the fort can be seen as dark cropmarks, while the lighter parchmark within represents stunted crop growth over the rampart of the fort. Parts of the metalled internal streets are also visible as parchmarks.

This site was first identified on an air photograph by Chris Balkwill in 1975. In the drought of 1984 the existence of a second ditch was observed for the first time, and further enclosures in the vicinity were identified from the air. Those to the north of the fort (left centre) are of unknown date, but that to the south is quite likely to be a small Roman fortlet. This is interesting because it may suggest two separate phases of Roman activity on the site. We are beginning to observe evidence of this type at many of the military sites in Dumnonia – for instance at Tiverton, the site opposite – and it is becoming clear that the Roman military occupation of south-west England was more complex than was once believed.

Further Reading

Balkwill, C.J. 'A Roman Site at Okehampton', *PDAS* 34 (1976), 89–92

Bidwell, P.T., Bridgwater, R. and Silvester, R.J. 'The Roman Fort at Okehampton, Devon', *Britannia* 10 (1979), 255–8

Griffith, F.M. 'Roman Military Sites in Devon: Some Recent Discoveries', *PDAS* 42 (1984), 11–32

Photograph: F.M. Griffith, Devon County Council, 26 June 1984

(Right) Plan of the principal features at Okehampton

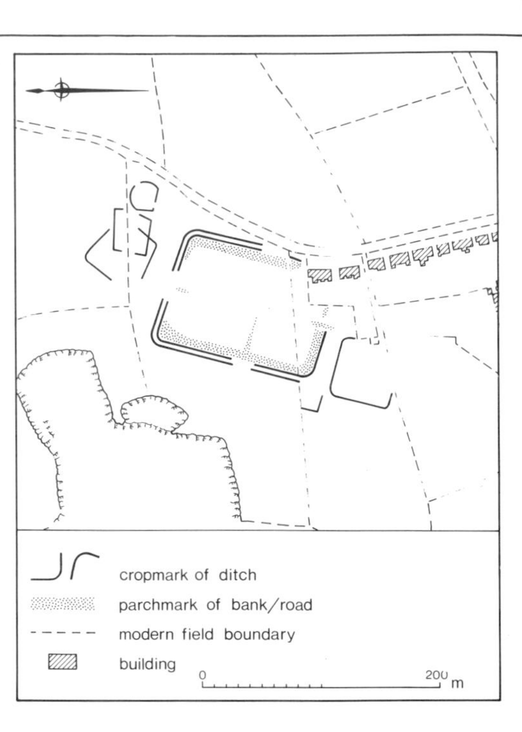

Plate 36

Excavations at the Roman Fort at Bolham, Tiverton

The Roman fort at Tiverton was discovered in 1978 by Andrew King in the course of a survey of the line of the proposed North Devon Link Road (which has since been built nearby, without disturbance to the fort). He identified the very faint soilmark of what was taken to be a Roman camp while examining aerial photographs taken in 1946.

The faintness of the mark suggested a fortification which, although rather slight, had the characteristic shape of a Roman military work, and this was initially thought to be a Roman 'marching camp' – a site built perhaps only for a one-night halt. Between 1981 and 1986 excavations at the west entrance were carried out by Dr Valerie Maxfield and the Tiverton Archaeological Group. These proved the site to be not a temporary camp but a regular fort dating from the third quarter of the first century A.D. The reason the defences gave such a slight indication of their presence was that the ditch had been deliberately backfilled with the clay of the rampart when the fort was decommissioned, so that there was little difference between the moisture-retaining properties of the ditch-fill, the rampart and the surrounding subsoil.

The excavation of the entrance identified two successive gate structures of different types. A gate composed of ten posts (two ranks of five, giving a double-portalled gate with flanking towers) was demolished and replaced with a nine-post structure (three rows of three with no flanking towers). The metalled road passing through the gate also showed evidence of several phases of use, while faint cropmarks in the environs of the fort observed in the drought of 1984 hint at other military works. While the fort was probably not continuously occupied, this evidence indicates that the site, which lies in a key position in the Exe valley, played a role in the army's operations in the South West for a considerable period of time. This information, with that from Okehampton and other sites, contributes to the slow process of building up a better picture of the activities of the Roman army in Dumnonia.

Further Reading

King, A.C. 'A Roman Marching Camp near Tiverton', *PDAS* 36 (1978), 254–6

Maxfield, V.A. 'The Army and the Land in the Roman South-west' in (ed.) Higham, R.A. *Security and Defence in South-west England Before 1800* (ESH 19, University of Exeter, 1987) 1–26

— 'Excavations at the Roman fort at Bolham, Tiverton', *PDAS* forthcoming

Photograph: F.M. Griffith, Devon County Council, 17 July 1986

Plates 37 and 38

The Axe Valley

This view is taken down the River Axe from a position above Colyford, looking south towards Lyme Bay. Seaton is on the right of the picture and Axmouth on the left. The estuary has changed considerably since the sixteenth century; it was an important harbour in the medieval period and probably as far back as Roman times. The presence of a Roman site at Honeyditches, Seaton, has been known since the eighteenth century; the discovery of a fine tessellated pavement in 1921 indicated that there was a villa here. More recent archaeological work on the site suggests the existence of a Roman military or maritime base at Seaton, and has also identified an important neolithic and Bronze Age settlement.

The reason for the postulated Roman naval establishment would have been to utilize the harbour for coastal traffic. The area of what is now flat dry land between Seaton church and the river was a sheltered anchorage in the Roman period, though we know from accounts in the historic period that the shingle bar across the harbour was starting to grow by about the beginning of the fifteenth century, causing silting and preventing access into the river. The mouths of the Rivers Otter and Sid suffered a similar fate at the same time. Strenuous attempts were made to prevent or circumvent the growth of the bar, but Axmouth's life as a commercial port was effectively finished, though a coastal fishery continued.

A saltworking industry was established on the Seaton side of the estuary in the late seventeenth century, but Domesday Book tells us that there had already been saltworkers in the area in Saxon times. After the silting up of the estuary had begun, saltmarshes became established in the shallow backwaters, and in time these were reclaimed to provide good grazing. The previous extent of the tidal range within the estuary is marked in the photograph by the characteristic patterns of the drainage channels of saltings (below).

At the mouth of the river, a road crosses it by means of a bridge. This is the earliest remaining concrete bridge in the country, and as such has been scheduled as an Ancient Monument.

Further Reading

Miles, H. 'The Honeyditches Roman Villa, Seaton', *Britannia* 8 (1977), 107–43

Parkinson, M. 'The Axe Estuary and its marshes', *TDA* 117 (1985), 19–62

Silvester, R.J. 'Excavations at Honeyditches Roman Villa, Seaton, in 1978', *PDAS* 39 (1981), 37–88

— 'Roman Seaton and the Axe', *Devon Archaeol.* 2 (1984), 25–8

Photograph: F.M. Griffith, Devon County Council, 9 December 1986

Seaton marshes: the possible site of a Roman harbour

Photograph: F.M. Griffith, Devon County Council, 19 December 1986

Plate 39

Old Burrow, Countisbury

This earthwork, in a commanding position on the north Devon coastal clifftop, together with a comparable one 18 km to the west at Martinhoe, was investigated in the early 1960s by Lady (Aileen) Fox and Professor W. Ravenhill of Exeter University. Both sites were coastal fortlets or watch posts of the Roman army, dating from the first century A.D., but interesting differences were found between them. Old Burrow appears to have been in use for only a limited period, and although it has a substantial gate structure with a tower above it, the excavators found no evidence for permanent buildings within the fortlet, indicating that perhaps it was used for tented accommodation only. At Martinhoe, on the other hand, traces of the foundations of timber buildings were identified in excavation, leading the excavators to suggest that this site was in use for a much longer period, possibly replacing the site at Old Burrow. Martinhoe lies in a much less exposed situation, but one which still allows a watch to be kept on shipping passing up the Bristol Channel. The fortlets would have formed part of the system of Roman frontier defences during the consolidation of their advance into the South West and Wales.

Further Reading

Fox, A. and Ravenhill, W.L.D. 'Early Roman Outposts on the North Devon Coast, Old Burrow and Martinhoe', *PDAS* 24 (1966), 3–39

Old Burrow DAS Field Guide (forthcoming)

Photograph: National Monuments Record, RCHME, 1 March 1979

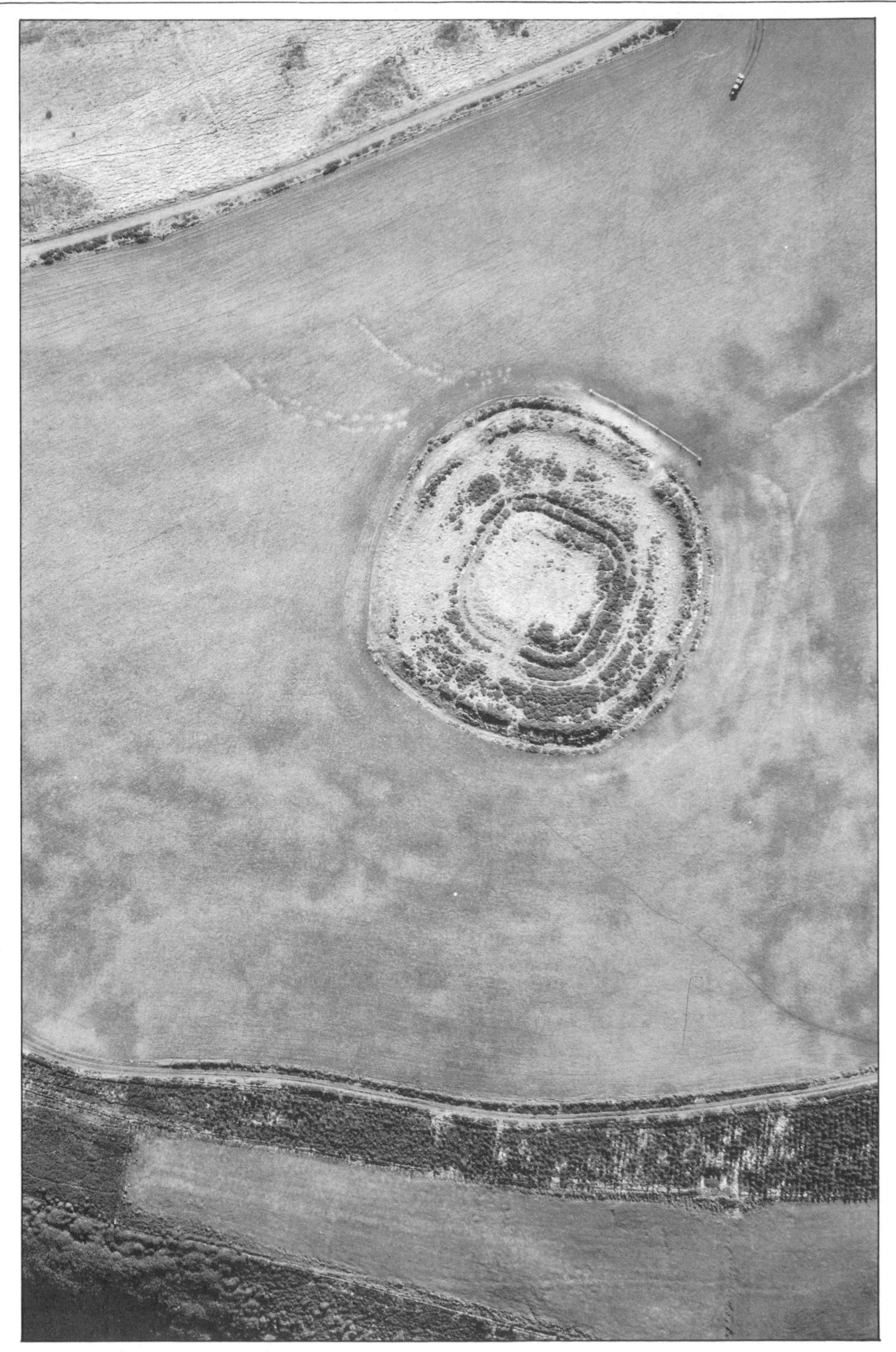

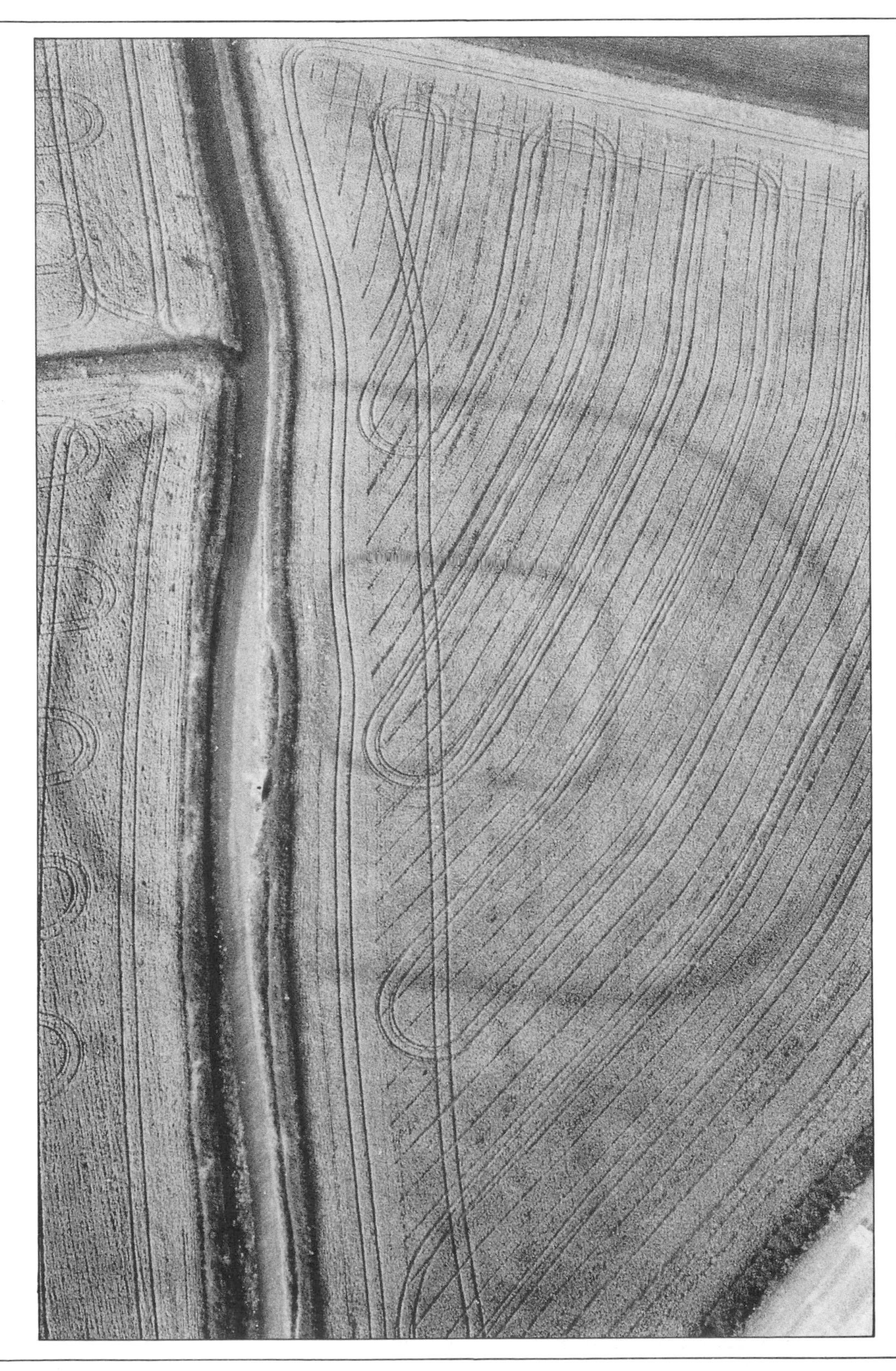

Plate 40

Possible Roman Signal Station or Fortlet near Exeter

This hilltop site, some 5 km south-west of Exeter, was observed as a cropmark for the first time during the drought of 1984, though a soilmark had previously been recorded. The general appearance of this site is comparable with that of Old Burrow (the preceding photograph) and it is also closely paralleled by the long-known double-ditched enclosure site, believed to be a first-century Roman military fortlet, at Stoke Hill, just to the north of Exeter. Both this and the Stoke Hill site are situated in strong hilltop positions, with good visibility all round and intervisibility between the two. Neither excavations at Stoke Hill nor fieldwalking on this site have produced much information in the form of finds; the explanation for this may be that both sites were very shortlived, possibly having a temporary role related to the legionary fortress at Exeter (p.48), which they both overlook.

Further Reading

Fox, A. and Ravenhill, W. 'The Stoke Hill Roman Signal Station', *TDA* 91 (1959), 71–82

Griffith, F.M. 'Roman Military Sites in Devon: Some Recent Discoveries', *PDAS* 42 (1984), 11–32 (with appendix on Stoke Hill by H. Quinnell)

Photograph: F.M. Griffith, Devon County Council, 7 July 1984

Plate 41

Line of probable Roman Road at Colebrooke

While we are now beginning to piece together some aspects of the Roman impact on the South West, one area where little progress has been made of late is in the identification of the road system. In other parts of the country the pursuit of Roman roads has long been a popular pastime, but in Devon roads are strangely elusive. Intelligent inference and chance finds enable us to postulate a number of the road lines with a fair degree of confidence – for example, the Exeter–Honiton part of the A30, or the general line of the road over Haldon towards Newton Abbot – but this is one aspect of study where the impact of aerial reconnaissance has been very slight. This is probably due to the conservatism of Devon road lines: the Roman roads are likely to be on the lines of prehistoric trackways, and directly underneath the present roads.

Shown here is part of a Roman road whose general course has been known for some time but whose line is still being elucidated in detail. This was the main route into Cornwall in the Roman period. It ran from Exeter past Crediton, westwards to the military complex at North Tawton, and then to the fort at Okehampton and on to Launceston. It is seen here just west of the River Troney near its confluence with the Yeo. The road can be seen running straight up the centre of the photograph: its line has been followed by some of the field boundaries, but, particularly where these have been removed, the parchmark of the buried road can be seen to be broader than the hedges themselves. (The herringbone pattern in the nearest field shows the layout of some field drains.) The road here runs up a spine of high ground between two small streams, and it diverges very little from this general orientation all the way westward to the fort at North Tawton. About one-third of the way up the picture a squarish field is seen set astride the road. It has been suggested that this could be a Roman military site, but no definite evidence has yet been found.

Further Reading

Lambert, M. J. 'Roads to the Roman Camp at North Tawton', *TDA* 105 (1973), 131–9

Margary, I.D. *Roman Roads in Britain* (revised ed. John Baker, 1967)

Stevens, C.E. 'The Sacred Wood' in (ed.) Megaw, J.V.S. *To Illustrate the Monuments: Essays Presented to Stuart Piggott* (Thames & Hudson, 1976), 240–44

Photograph: F.M. Griffith, Devon County Council, 19 March 1986

A Romano-British Farm at Stoke Gabriel

Many of the 'new' archaeological sites discovered in the last few years are seen only as the square or subrectangular ditch that surrounded a settlement or farmstead, now observable only in exceptional conditions (see below). This photograph shows a rare example of such a farmstead still surviving in part in above-ground form. Around the central enclosure where the farmstead itself was probably situated, the banks forming the edges of small fields can be seen in the photograph. Previously these survived in the surrounding modern fields as well, but their traces have now been removed by ploughing.

The site was excavated in 1955 by the late E.N. Masson Phillips, and was shown to have been occupied in the Romano-British period, from the first to the fourth century A.D. Among the finds were a *fibula* or brooch, and pottery manufactured in south Devon, other parts of Britain, and imported from Gaul. The enclosure itself, which unusually was dug into the limestone bedrock (see p.45), had been in use for only a short period of time before its ditch was allowed to fill up. The rock in the sides of the ditch was found to be fresh and unweathered when excavated. This may suggest some early change in the function or defensive requirements of the site after the construction of the enclosure.

A similar site, recorded as a roughly square cropmark, has recently been excavated in east Devon and proved to be of the same general date. Many of the other known cropmark enclosures may well turn out to represent sites like this, but few firm conclusions can be drawn about their function and date until a much wider range has been excavated.

Further Reading

Griffith, F.M. and Robinson, R. 'Enclosures in the South Hams', *PDAS* forthcoming

— in (ed.) Timms, S.C. *Archaeology of the Devon Landscape,* forthcoming

Masson Phillips, E.N. 'Excavation of a Romano-British Site at Lower Well Farm, Stoke Gabriel, Devon', *PDAS* 23 (1966), 3–34

Photograph: F.M. Griffith, Devon County Council, 23 December 1986

Plate 43–48

Settlements known from cropmark evidence

As mentioned above, most sites similar to that at Stoke Gabriel no longer exhibit any above-ground traces of their existence. In the past, this led archaeologists to believe that much of lowland Devon was only very sparsely inhabited during the prehistoric and Romano-British periods. Recent aerial reconnaissance has identified numerous previously unrecorded enclosures, many of which probably represent settlements, in all parts of lowland Devon. Analysis of the large number of sites recorded as cropmarks in recent years is still in progress, and the conclusions to be drawn are at present limited by the absence of dating evidence for the majority of the enclosures. While it is possible to identify some types of archaeological site, such as a Roman fort (plate 35) or a henge (plate 9), from their distinctive appearance with a fair degree of confidence, the enclosures, whose only visible feature is usually the line of their perimeter ditch, share too restricted a range of morphological characteristics to allow firm attribution of date or function at present. (These problems are discussed in more detail in the Introduction.) The few cropmark enclosures that have so far been excavated in the South West have principally proved to be of Romano-British date, but, on the basis of results from elsewhere in the country, many of the other sites are likely to be considerably earlier. Almost certainly some of the enclosures already recorded in Devon date back to the Neolithic and Bronze Age periods, and a wide range of functions is likely to be concealed among the apparently simple range of shapes.

Air photography can generally identify only those

Plate 43 The site shown in plate 44 occupies a gentle hollow, and a low rise shows the last trace of its bank on the ground.
Photograph: Rosemary Robinson, 1 September 1987

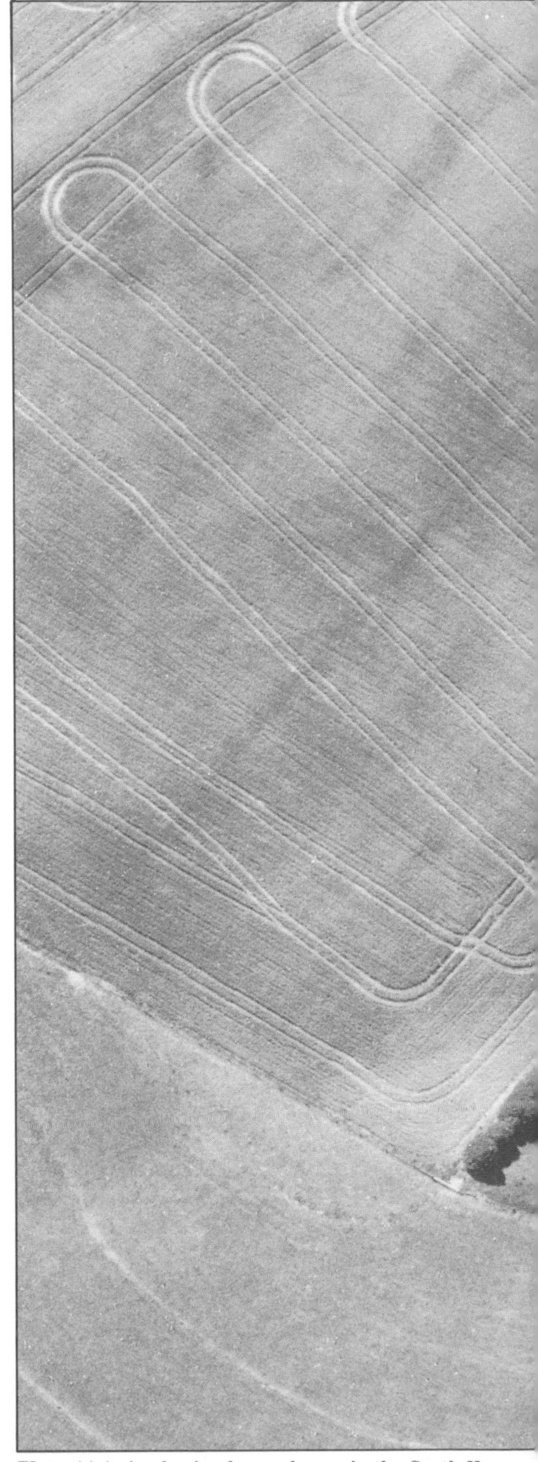

Plate 44 A simple circular enclosure in the South Hams.
Photograph: F.M. Griffith, Devon County Council, 11 July 1984

settlements which are defined by a surrounding ditch and/or bank, and unenclosed settlements usually require the use of other survey techniques for their recognition. More excavations will be needed to date the range of sites observed: their discovery from the air is only the first, albeit essential, stage in understanding them. At least once they have been located proper provision can be made for preservation or rescue excavation if they are threatened by development (see plate 31), and such excavation will in turn provide further information on their date and function.

The enclosures so far recorded through aerial photography fall into a limited range of shapes and sizes, from almost completely circular (plate 44) to strictly rectangular with sharp corners (plate 45). The analysis which is now being undertaken will examine not only their morphological features but also their topographical siting, their access to natural resources, the geological base and the soils on which they are situated and their field remains and finds. Only further work will help clarify whether the apparently distinct groups of characteristics identified represent significant and discrete classes of sites. More complex shapes have also been recognized: that represented by the site in plate 46 is a type that recurs in several different areas. (There are of course particular problems in the interpretation of multiple-ditched enclosures; unless, as here, the ditches appear to be actually linked together, it is often impossible to say from the photograph whether we are seeing a single double-ditched enclosure or one single-ditched one replacing another on the same site.)

The enclosure shown in plate 47 illustrates the necessity of a field visit to understand the topography of a site properly. The air photograph inevitably 'flattens out' topographical features, and even a large-scale map does not record the subtleties of the lie of the land in sufficient detail. This enclosure is triple-ditched, at least in part, but at the left-hand side of the photograph, in the corner of the field, it has a multiplicity of short lengths of ditch outside it. A field visit suggested the reason for these: the site lies in a strong position just off the top of a long ridge (the lane in the picture runs along the ridge top) and the enclosure occupies the only flatter area on the hillside, with the ground falling away steeply on two sides. On the left-hand side, however, the enclosure is approached by a small subsidiary ridge of gentler slope (which shows as a paler area in the crop on the photograph). It is this comparatively vulnerable access point that the proliferation of ditches here was probably designed to protect. This particular enclosure, therefore, appears to be built with greater regard to the site's defensive potential than the majority of the enclosures so far recorded. There are very few of the recently identified cropmark enclosures whose siting cannot be elucidated to some

Plate 45 A hillslope enclosure with sharply angled corners situated on the north side of the Dart valley. Other cropmark enclosures can be seen in the background.
Photograph: F.M. Griffith, Devon County Council, 11 July 1984

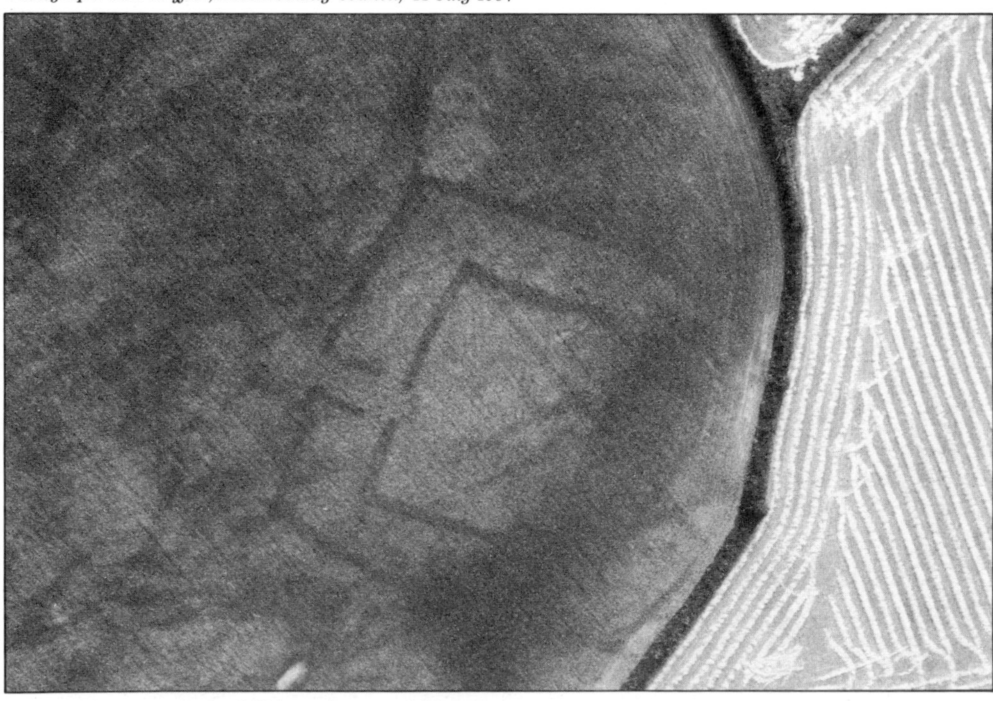

Plate 46 A more complex hillslope site near Ashburton.
Note how the present-day hedge appears to observe the boundary of the enclosure (cf. plate 28).
Photograph: F.M. Griffith, Devon County Council, 20 July 1984

extent by inspection in the field. The small circular enclosure (plate 44) proved, for example, on field inspection to occupy a slight hollow in the hillside (plate 43).

Recent work undertaken both by aerial archaeologists and by those carrying out detailed fieldwalking projects is transforming the archaeological picture of the settlement and the level of exploitation of lowland Devon in the prehistoric and Romano-British periods. Much further work is needed before we can adequately interpret the implications of the results of recent work and construct updated models of the way the landscape was used in each period, but this will provide a stimulating and challenging archaeological problem in the coming years.

Further Reading

For more information on cropmarks in general, the reader is referred to the Bibliography at the beginning of this book.

Plate 47 Complex enclosure on the side of a ridge, north of Teignmouth. Note the multiple additional ditch lengths on the least steep side.
Photograph: F.M. Griffith, 18 July 1983

Plate 48 Cropmarks do not appear only in the summer. This curvilinear enclosure is revealed by enhanced growth in a root crop in November.
Photograph: F.M. Griffith, Devon County Council, 23 November 1987

Plate 49

Bantham Ham, South Devon

Bantham Ham is an area of sand-dunes overlying folded slates and shales at the mouth of the River Avon in south Devon. In some conditions a storm can change the shape of these dunes completely, or strip bare an area previously sand-covered. From time to time deposits of bone and pottery have been exposed in the dunes by such storms, and examination of finds collected by local fieldworkers over a number of years enabled Lady (Aileen) Fox to identify this site as one in use during the post-Roman or Dark Age period – around the fifth to eighth centuries A.D. It appears to have been an occupation site, but perhaps was only seasonally used. A number of similar sites have been recognized around the coasts of Cornwall and Wales; how many there originally were is unknown, since their discovery is so much a matter of chance. Many will doubtless have been lost entirely, either through coastal erosion or through 'development' of the seaside area. These coastal sites are of importance since inland settlements of the period are extraordinarily hard to locate, though they certainly existed. Much of what we know of south-west England in the Dark Ages derives from examination of coastal sites, and it is a problem for archaeologists to know how they related to the totality of the post-Roman economy.

Further Reading

Fox, A. 'Some evidence for a Dark Age Trading Site at Bantham, near Thurlestone, South Devon', *Antiq. J.* 35 (1955), 55–67

Griffith, F.M. 'Salvage Observations at Bantham Ham, Devon', *PDAS* 44 (1986), 39–58

Silvester, R.J. 'An Excavation on the Post-Roman Site at Bantham, South Devon', *PDAS* 39 (1981), 89–118

Photograph: F.M. Griffith, Devon County Council, 6 March 1986

Plate 50

High Peak, East Devon

This spectacular site, at High Peak on the east Devon cliffs beyond Otterton, was first recognized as being of archaeological significance by General Simcoe (who later became Governor of Canada) in the late eighteenth century. Since then more of the site has been lost to the sea, and in the 1840s the antiquary P.O. Hutchinson recorded finding charcoal and bone deposits eroding from the cliff face. Only a small proportion of the original area now survives.

The site consists of a segment of earthwork fortifications cutting off the highest part of the cliff top. The ground slopes steeply up to this point, and with the sea on the southern side it nowadays gives the impression of being a very strong defensible site. It has recently been suggested, however, that so much has been lost through erosion in this area that the site may not originally have been situated on the clifftop at all, but on a hill lying slightly back from the coast.

The earthworks at High Peak were long thought to be those of an Iron Age hillfort-type site, but Mrs Pollard, the site's most recent excavator, concluded that they date from its Dark Age phase of occupation. At that time – probably the sixth to eighth centuries A.D. – the defended enclosure at High Peak seems to have been a fairly high-status site, as, for example, imported Mediterranean wine amphorae have been found there. The essential insecurity of existence at this time is however suggested by the exploitation of such a forbidding location. Radiocarbon dating and flint and pottery finds have shown that this point was also occupied in the fourth millennium B.C., perhaps as a stronghold comparable with Hembury (plate 8), and subsequently in the Roman period, possibly as one of a series of coastal observation posts like Old Burrow (plate 39). High Peak is a landmark visible from many places in east Devon, which would have been ideal for this purpose. It probably subsequently served as a beacon site for the same reason.

Further Reading

Burrow, I.C.G. 'Dark Age Devon: The Landscape A.D. 400–1100' in (ed.) Timms, S.C. *Archaeology of the Devon Landscape* (Devon County Council, 1980), 63–70

Pollard, S.H.M. 'Neolithic and Dark Age Settlements on High Peak, Sidmouth, Devon', *PDAS* 23 (1966), 35–59

Photograph: F.M. Griffith, 29 October 1983

Plate 51

Lundy, Bristol Channel

The island of Lundy lies in the entrance to the Bristol Channel, about 18 km NNW of Hartland Point. It is the only place in Devon where granite sea-cliffs are to be seen. They rise steeply out of the sea on almost all sides of the island giving few landing places. Nevertheless there is evidence of human activity on Lundy from the Mesolithic period onwards, and the cairns, round houses and extensive field systems which still survive suggest a thriving community in the later prehistoric period. However, it is perhaps Dark Age Lundy that strikes the visitor most today.

On Beacon Hill, the highest point on the island (just visible in the middle of the island on this photograph, taken from the south), there are the well-preserved remains of a Dark Age cemetery. Excavations here in the 1960s showed that the graveyard, possibly of the enclosed type that in Cornwall would be called a *lan,* was created in land previously in cultivation. It had as its focus in the Early Christian period (fifth to seventh centuries A.D.) a 'tomb-shrine' of three graves enclosed by upright slabs of granite and perhaps originally covered by a cairn. The cemetery enclosure can still be seen on Beacon Hill, and within it three splendid examples of Early Christian memorial stones: either grave markers or free-standing memorials, each with the name of the person commemorated inscribed in the granite in Latin. Such memorial stones are a characteristic element of Early Christian society in the Celtic west of Britain: the use of Latin continued in the early Church and the chiefly society of the west long before the conversion of Anglo-Saxon eastern England by Augustine and his followers. Finds from excavations elsewhere on Lundy of imported Mediterranean pottery like that from Bantham and High Peak give clues to the lifestyle of the occupants of the island at this time.

The position that Lundy occupies at the mouth of the Bristol Channel has made it useful for a variety of purposes in the past, varying from a base for pirates to military use for post-mediaeval gun batteries. In the nineteenth century, at the peak of the prosperity of Swansea, Cardiff, Bristol and Gloucester in both the transatlantic and coastal trades, it was estimated that over one million shipping movements passed Lundy every year. The lighthouse here was consequently a most important navigation feature in the channel. Also in the modern period, the granite quarries of the eastern side of Lundy exported stone in large quantities, including that used for the Thames embankment in London.

Further Reading

Chanter, J. R. *Lundy Island* (1877)
Gardner, K.S. *Lundy, an Archaeological Field Guide* (Lundy Field Society, n.d., circa 1983)
Langham, A.H. *Lundy* (1970) (David & Charles, 1984)
Pearce, S.M. *The Kingdom of Dumnonia* (Lodenek Press, Padstow, 1978)
Thomas, C. *Britain and Ireland in Early Christian Times* (Oxford University Press, 1971)

Photograph: F.M. Griffith, Devon County Council, 9 July 1987

Plate 52

Brent Tor, West Devon

The hill of Brent Tor – a landmark visible for many miles around – is a knoll formed by intrusive igneous rocks projecting through and above the surrounding flat lands of west Devon. Such a prominent feature is likely always to have provided a focus for human activity. In the first millennium B.C. the natural defensive advantages of the site were exploited when earthwork ramparts running around the contour towards the base of the hill were constructed to provide the defences for a hillfort. These can be seen on the photograph in the foreground.

Subsequently, the hill was used for the construction of the church of Brentor parish by the abbots of Tavistock. The volcanic rock of the hill itself was used for the church, which, like many churches in a similar situation is dedicated to St Michael. The hilltop almost certainly served as a beacon point as well, one in a chain of such sites running along the side of Dartmoor and it was also the site of a mediaeval fair. Brentor provides an excellent example of an isolated Devon parish church: the parish does not really have a village at its core, and although there is a chapel of ease, Christ Church, at North Brentor, this hamlet was historically in Lamerton parish and was not added to Brentor until 1880.

Further Reading

Burton, C.K. and Matthews, G.L., *The Church of St Michael, Brentor* (published privately, 1981)

Hine, J. 'St. Michael's, Brentor', *TDA* 1 pt 5 (1866), 116–21

Silvester, R.J. 'The Relationship of First Millennium Settlement to the Upland Areas of the South-West', *PDAS* 37 (1979), 176–90

Photograph: J.K.S. St Joseph, Cambridge University, 25 June 1955 (Crown copyright)

Plate 53

Crediton Parish Church

Crediton parish church occupies the site of a minster church founded in the early eighth century from Sherborne Abbey. In 909, when a separate diocese for Devon and Cornwall was created, Crediton became the seat of the bishop, and remained so until the see was moved to Exeter in 1050. There is a tradition that St Boniface, the seventh-century English missionary to Germany, was born in Crediton.

Excavations in 1984 in the vicarage garden (the trench can be seen at the top of the photograph as a red patch in the garden) located part of a timber building of Anglo-Saxon or early Norman date. Well-preserved waterlogged deposits of the same date were discovered in the little valley between the church and the vicarage. This is of great archaeological interest as it offers hope for the eventual recovery of more information on the early minster and its community.

In the post-Conquest period Crediton continued to be episcopal property and the large church and parish were served by a college of canons until the Dissolution. The church is built of the local New Red Sandstone; while the earliest parts of the existing fabric date from the twelfth century, most of it is fifteenth-century work, retaining the Norman cruciform plan.

The churchyard at Crediton is a splendid example of a parish graveyard. Its extension toward the vicarage in the nineteenth century occasioned the demolition of the mediaeval Vicars Choral buildings which had survived until then, but fragments of other parts of the collegiate buildings may yet be identified in excavation.

East Street, running across the bottom of the picture, forms the backbone of the long straggling borough of Crediton, which was formerly in two separate parts, East Town and West Town. The shape of Crediton is largely dictated by this road which runs along the sandstone ridge, the burgage plots stretching back on either side.

Further Reading

Orme, N. 'The Church in Crediton from St Boniface to the Reformation' in (ed.) Reuter, T. *The Greatest Englishman* (Paternoster Press, 1980)

Timms, S.C. 'Historic Towns in Devon' in (ed.) Timms, S.C. *Archaeology of the Devon Landscape* (Devon County Council, 1980), 97–110

Weddell, P.J. 'Excavations at Crediton in 1984 and 1986', *PDAS* forthcoming

Photograph: F.M. Griffith, Devon County Council, 26 July 1984

Plate 54

The Anglo-Saxon *Burh* at Lydford

Three of the four Burghal Hidage *burhs* of Devon (see also p.71) were at Halwell (near Totnes, which succeeded it), Exeter and Barnstaple/Pilton (plates 56 and 57). The fourth was at *Hlidan,* a place usually, in spite of some philological problems, identified with Lydford, where we know there was a later Anglo-Saxon mint. The position of Lydford is admirable in defensive terms: it lies on a steep spur formed by a bend in the River Lyd. The only side lacking natural defences, the north-east, was protected in the late Saxon period by a massive earthen bank, which can still be seen on the ground and in the photograph (right centre). A date in the 880s, in the reign of King Alfred, is the most probable for the construction of these defences, which are similar to those of other known promontory *burhs*. The town's layout, too, is thought by many to preserve another characteristic feature of planned late Saxon towns: a regular gridded street pattern (quite unlike the layout of, for example, Totnes, plate 73). Parts of this street layout have been identified in excavations carried out in the 1960s by Peter Addyman, and he has suggested that elements of this formal layout may still be observed in the present-day pattern of lanes and paths.

By the time of the Norman Conquest Lydford was an important town: Domesday Book records that it paid as much towards military expeditions as Barnstaple or Totnes. Domesday Book also gives us a clue to the date of the first Norman castle in Lydford when it records that forty houses had been 'laid waste' there since the Conquest. This may in part represent houses destroyed in the construction of the early 'ringwork' castle or fort that can be seen in the upper left of the picture. This fort was later superseded by a stone castle which itself was rebuilt in the second part of the thirteenth century as the keep visible in the centre of the picture – later to become the infamous stannary prison. By 1300, however, Lydford was falling behind in the league of successful Devon towns, having only forty-eight burgesses, for example, when Totnes had some 350. Lydford's relative inaccessibility meant that it could not compete with Okehampton or Tavistock as a market centre. It is to this early commercial failure that we owe the excellent and visible preservation of the Anglo-Saxon and Norman town's defences and other features, which at more successful towns have to be reconstructed by archaeological and topographical detective work.

Further Reading

Higham, R.A. 'Public and Private Defence in the Medieval South West: Town, Castle and Fort' in (ed.) Higham, R.A. *Security and Defence in South-West England before 1800* (ESH 19, University of Exeter, 1987), 27–50

Saunders, A. 'Lydford Castle, Devon', *Med. Archaeol.* 24 (1980), 123–86

— *Lydford Saxon Town and Castle* (HMSO, 1982) (Guide available in Lydford)

Timms, S.C. 'The Royal Town of Lydford', *Devon Archaeol.* 3 (1985), 19–23

Photograph: F.M. Griffith, Devon County Council, 20 June 1984

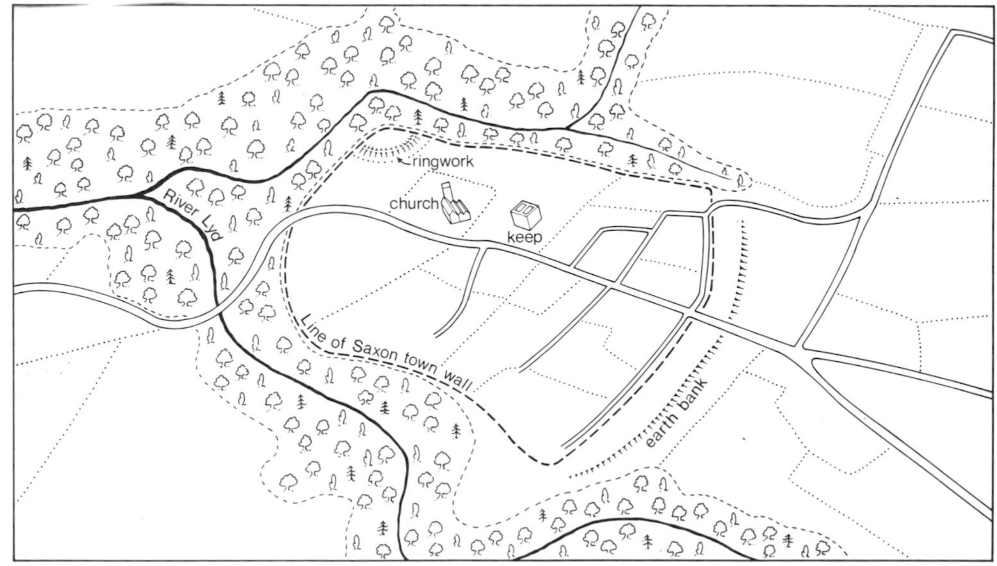

Plate 55

Berry Camp, Branscombe

Berry Camp is situated on the clifftop on the east Devon coast between High Peak (plate 50) and Beer Head (plate 7). It is a large defensible hilltop enclosure, part of which has been lost through cliff erosion. Although it has never been tested by excavation, the site is believed to date from the earlier first millennium B.C.

Many defended sites in Devon are called 'Berry' or 'Bury Castle' or similar names: in this book two Hembury Castles are illustrated, one in east Devon and one in the south; there is another one still in Buckland Brewer parish west of the River Torridge, while plate 29 shows an 'Embury'. These sites and many more have names deriving from the Anglo-Saxon word *burh* (not to be confused with *beorg,* which gives us the modern word 'barrow'). *Burh* has a wide range of meanings, from a simple domestic enclosure to a defended town like Lydford; cognate words continued in use in Middle English. The word seems to have been used by speakers of Anglo-Saxon both to describe any pre-existing defensive site they encountered, and also for enclosures they built themselves.

It is possible to postulate the existence of a site from place-name evidence alone, and this is sometimes done, for example, by historians in the reconstruction of Anglo-Saxon charter boundaries from the landmark points named therein. On the other hand, the discovery of an enclosure site as a cropmark may allow the tentative identification of a known but unlocated place-name: this has been possible for a number of the cropmark enclosures recently found in Devon, and some hitherto unexplained 'berry' place-names have now been provisionally located. The smaller picture shows a rectilinear cropmark enclosure of unknown date near Kingsbridge. The traces of former field boundaries can be seen running across it: these fields are named on the Tithe Apportionment of 1840 as Corner Thornberry, Little Thornberry, Long Thornberry and Great Thornberry. No explanation for these names had previously been available: the newly discovered enclosure offers one. The use of place-name evidence cannot in itself date a site, but at least it indicates that a site, perhaps now destroyed, was visible as an upstanding feature at the time the Anglo-Saxons were naming their landscape – that is, it gives us both a *terminus ante quem* for the construction of the earthwork, and a *terminus post quem* for its destruction.

Photograph: F.M. Griffith, Devon County Council, 19 December 1985

Photograph: F.M. Griffith, Devon County Council, 19 July 1984

Further Reading

Gelling, M. *Signposts to the Past* (rev. ed. Phillimore, 1988)

Gover, J.E.B., Mawer, A. and Stenton, F.M. *Place-Names of Devon* (EPNS 8 and 9, 1931–2)

Griffith, F.M. '*Burh* and *Beorg* in Devon', *Nomina* 10 (1986), 93–103

Smith, A.H. *English Place-Name Elements* (EPNS 25 and 26, 1970)

Plate 56

Roborough Castle, North Devon

This hilltop is the site of an earthwork known as Burridge Camp or Roborough Castle. It is a rectangular defended enclosure for which the term 'hillfort' might be used; about 350 m to the east there is an outer defence to the enclosure in the form of a cross-ridge earthwork bank. This site has never been excavated, and no definite date for it is known.

The particular interest of this enclosure, however, lies in the fact that it has been suggested as the original site of the Saxon *burh* of Pilton, which is mentioned in the Anglo-Saxon *Burghal Hidage* – a document describing the arrangements King Alfred made for the defence of various forts and towns in southern England against the Danes. The *burh* of Pilton is believed to have been the predecessor of mediaeval Barnstaple. The circumference of Roborough Castle is roughly the same as that given in the *Burghal Hidage,* but the identification of this site with the *burh* of Pilton is far from universally accepted. Some authorities have located the *burh* further down the hill in modern Pilton, some at the site of Barnstaple itself (as one manuscript of the *Burghal Hidage* suggests), while others point out that the place-name 'Pilton' is a common one on the coast, and doubt that the name can be attributed with any certainty.

The names 'Burridge' and 'Roborough' are yet more variants on the 'Berry' names discussed above. Unfortunately the applications of the word *burh* appear to be so wide that the word could in this case mean the Saxon *burh* site that we are looking for here, or an existing Iron Age site refortified by the Saxons, or just a long-abandoned Iron Age earthwork observed in the landscape by Anglo-Saxon speaking settlers.

Further Reading

Hill, D.H. 'The Burghal Hidage; the Establishment of a text', *Med. Archaeol.* 13 (1969), 84–92

Miles, H. and T. 'Pilton, North Devon: Excavations within a Medieval Village', *PDAS* 33 (1975), 267–95

Whybrow, C. 'Some Multivallate Hill-Forts on Exmoor and in North Devon', *PDAS* 25 (1967), 1–18

Photograph: F.M. Griffith, Devon County Council, 30 January 1987

Plate 57

Barnstaple

The date of the origin of the *burh* at 'Pilton' has been discussed above. There is, however, no doubt that, wherever Pilton lay, Barnstaple itself was in existence as a defended *burh* well before the Norman Conquest, with its own mint by the mid tenth century. Excavations in the bailey of the Norman castle (the tree-covered mound centre right in the photograph) revealed a large pre-Norman graveyard that had been in use for a considerable period before the building of the castle. The castle is thought to have been constructed either at the time of the Conquest or in the early twelfth century. The line of the town defences can be seen reflected in the sweep of present-day Boutport ('round the town') Street (cf. Totnes, plate 73).

Barnstaple is strategically sited at the junction of the Rivers Taw (on the right) and Yeo (at the bottom of the picture). The flat area to the right of the castle is more recently reclaimed ground: originally the castle would have been almost at the edge of the river, its moat filled by the tide. Throughout the town the ordered layout of the burgage plots is clear: towards the top of the enclosed area the handsome nineteenth-century market building can be seen fitted into this pattern. At the top right, the Long Bridge is seen: the fabric of the present bridge dates mainly from the sixteenth century, but there was probably a timber bridge here in Saxon times. In the foreground boats and warehouses on the Yeo reflect Barnstaple's past importance as a major trading port. The town's Port Books record a flourishing trade, while ceramics from the famous Barnstaple Potteries were being traded throughout the New World by the seventeenth century. The centre of the pottery industry was Potters' Lane, which lies in front of the castle mound in this picture. Since this photograph was taken, the old Workhouse building, more recently Dornat's factory – the square structure of four ranges next to the castle – has been demolished and the new county library built. Excavations on the library site identified seventeenth-century potters' workshops and kilns here; further archaeological investigations will need to be undertaken as other sites in the heart of the area of the ceramic industry are redeveloped.

Further Reading

Farrell, T. 'Barnstaple', *Devon Archaeol.* 2 (1984), 1–6

Grant, A. *North Devon Pottery: the Seventeenth Century* (University of Exeter, 1983)

Haslam, J. 'The Towns of Devon' in (ed.) Haslam, J. *Anglo-Saxon Towns in Southern England* (Phillimore, 1984), 249–83

Higham, R.A. 'Barnstaple Castle', *Devon Archaeol.* 2 (1984) 7–9

Lamplugh, L. *Barnstaple, Town on the Taw* (Phillimore, 1983)

Miles, H. and T. 'Pilton, North Devon: Excavations within a Medieval Village', *PDAS* 33 (1975), 267–96

Miles, T.J. 'The Excavation of a Saxon Cemetery and part of the Norman Castle at North Walk, Barnstaple', *PDAS* 44 (1986), 59–84

Photograph: F.M. Griffith, Devon County Council, 18 August 1984

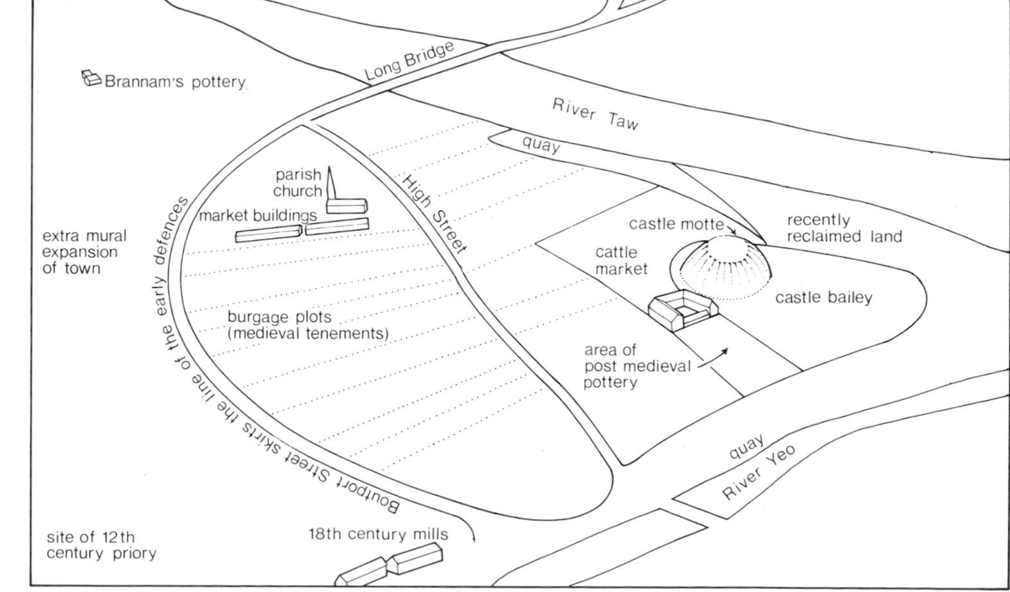

Plate 58

Loddiswell Rings

This impressive monument, also known as Blackdown Camp, lies on a gentle rise to the west of the Avon valley, commanding extensive views on all sides over the South Hams. The site has never been subjected to excavation, so statements about its date and purpose are based on interpretation of the field evidence alone. This suggests that we are looking at a monument of two main periods: its form and situation imply that it was originally an Iron Age hillfort, defended by a bank and ditch with counterscarp bank on the outside. Subsequently, at the Norman Conquest, a castle was constructed within the enclosure, making use of the hillfort defences to serve as an outer bailey. The inner bailey was tucked into the north-west corner of the hillfort, while the hollow-centred earthen mound within it surrounded the actual castle (perhaps only a single timber tower).

That a pre-existing defended site was chosen for this Norman castle may only reflect the fact that a good defensible position is attractive to military people of all periods, but it also suggests that this may be one of the earlier castles of the Norman Conquest, when the rapid utilization of an existing earthwork made good sense in the circumstances of the time. This was often the practice when the Normans took over an Anglo-Saxon town, as at Rougemont Castle in Exeter and the early castle at Lydford, but it is also paralleled in a rural context at Hembury Castle, Buckfastleigh (fig. 3 in the Introduction), where a motte again occupies part of a hillfort interior.

Outside the hillfort on the south and east sides a series of low terraces and platforms may be seen, perhaps indicating traces of some settlement outside the defended enclosure itself, as is often the case with Norman castles.

Further Reading

Higham, R.A. 'Castles in Devon' in (ed.) Timms, S.C. *Archaeology of the Devon Landscape* (Devon County Council, 1980) 71–80

— 'Public and Private Defence in the Medieval South West: Town, Castle and Fort' in (ed.) Higham, R.A. *Security and Defence in South-West England before 1800* (ESH 19, University of Exeter, 1987), 27–50

Photograph: F.M. Griffith, Devon County Council, 6 March 1986

Plate 59

Holwell Castle, Parracombe

Seen from the air the situation of Holwell Castle does not look particularly strong. On the ground, however, it can be seen to occupy a perfectly defensible position on the spur formed by the confluence of two streams. This is a common siting for a motte and bailey castle of this type.

The only excavation carried out at Holwell took place in 1905, so information on its construction is limited. It is a good example of the many small and probably fairly short-lived defended sites for which no contemporary documentation is available. We know, however, that Holwell was part of the estate of William de Falaise, one of William I's tenants-in-chief in 1086. A date for the castle either in the early years of the Norman Conquest or perhaps in the Civil War of the twelfth century has been suggested by Robert Higham.

Holwell shows clearly the two main elements of these smaller castles: the motte or earthen mound upon which the principal building was sited, and the bailey – the area enclosed by a bank to provide additional defensible space. Some castles were constructed with two or more baileys: there is some evidence for an outer bailey at Barnstaple, and we have seen how an earlier earthwork was exploited to serve as an outer bailey at Loddiswell (plate 58). No masonry traces survive at Holwell, but fragments of roofing slate have been found. It is probable that this was one of the numerous timber castles built at this time, whose construction would have required the use of rather fewer resources than even quite a small stone castle.

Further Reading

Higham, R.A. 'Castles in Devon' in (ed.) Timms, S.C. *Archaeology of the Devon Landscape* (Devon County Council, 1980) 71–80

— 'Public and Private Defence in the Medieval South West: Town, Castle and Fort' in (ed.) Higham, R.A. *Security and Defence in South-West England before 1800* (ESH 19, University of Exeter, 1987), 27–50

Photograph: F.M. Griffith, Devon County Council, 30 January 1987

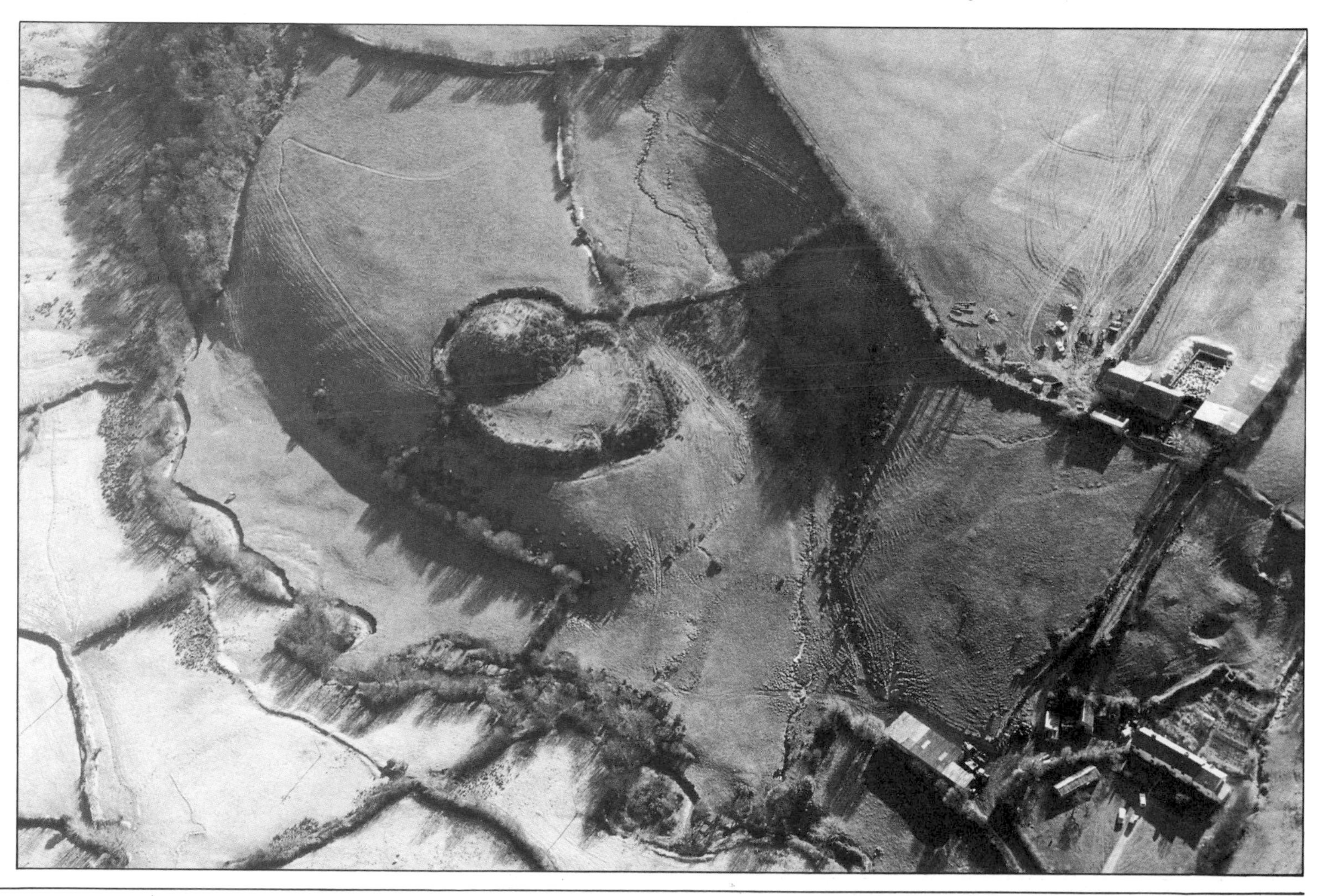

Plate 60

Okehampton Castle

This photograph shows another of the castles erected by the Normans soon after the Conquest. Okehampton is in fact the only Devon castle specifically mentioned in Domesday Book in 1086. Unlike the castles at Exeter, Lydford, Totnes and Barnstaple, it was established on a 'green field' site in a rural manor. The castle was built by Baldwin de Brionne, William's most powerful baron in Devon and royal sheriff of the county, who had also been partly responsible for the building of Exeter Castle and who was in possession of nearly 200 manors in Devon by 1086.

Although the motte and the western defences were first built in the immediate post-Conquest period, the castle as we see it now is almost entirely the result of a major rebuilding undertaken in the early fourteenth century by Hugh, a member of the powerful Devon family of the Courtenays, and the first Courtenay Earl of Devon. The keep on the motte was extensively altered to provide a building of more domestic character, and most of the present structures in the bailey were erected at that time.

The photograph shows the castle from the west. The motte, surmounted by its keep, is in the foreground, and to the left is the bailey, surrounded by a curtain wall and containing the castle's domestic buildings – the Great Hall, kitchen, chapel and lodgings. Beyond the bailey can be seen the barbican or fortified entrance passage, an easily controlled corridor between an outer and an inner gatehouse.

In spite of its strongly fortified appearance there is no evidence that Okehampton was ever involved in active warfare. It served during the Middle Ages as an administrative centre for the large estates of its successive powerful owners, and as a rural retreat and hunting lodge for its lords (see opposite). After 1539, when its then owner, Henry, Marquess of Exeter, was executed and his estates forfeited to the Crown, most of the buildings of the castle fell into decay or were dismantled, and it never again served as a prestige residence. By the seventeenth century it is recorded in such mundane uses as a bakehouse.

Further Reading

Higham, R.A. 'Excavations at Okehampton Castle, Devon, Part 1: the Motte and Keep', *PDAS* 35 (1977), 3–42

Higham, R.A., Allan, J.P. and Blaylock, S.R. 'Excavations at Okehampton Castle, Devon, Part 2: The Bailey', *PDAS* 40 (1982), 19–152

Higham, R.A. *Okehampton Castle* (HMSO Official Handbook, 1984)

Photograph: F.M. Griffith, Devon County Council, 9 September 1986

Plate 61

Okehampton Park

At or before the beginning of the fourteenth century, Hugh Courtenay, whose rebuilding of Okehampton Castle is mentioned above, established a deer park on the northern flank of Dartmoor on the opposite side of the West Okement River from his castle. This was to provide himself and his guests with sport in hunting deer when they were staying at the castle. Recent excavations at the castle have produced evidence in the form of bones that the native stock of red deer was replaced by imported fallow deer in around 1300, presumably for the sake of the hunting. The boundary of the park may have been the same as the large enclosure which can still be made out on the map today, although there is no documentary evidence for the existence of this enclosure earlier than the eighteenth century. Parts of the present park have been obliterated by the army camp at the east and the ballast quarry at the west (beyond the lower left-hand corner of the picture).

Within the park the upstanding remains of a number of scattered mediaeval farmsteads survive, similar to those at Houndtor (page 79). This photograph shows the curvilinear enclosures of a number of small farmsteads scattered among the fields.

In 1976–8 two groups of these buildings were excavated before their destruction by the expansion of the quarry. They proved to be fairly shortlived farming settlements, practising mixed farming with an arable component; the ridge and furrow on the photograph appears to relate to these farms. They were probably first built in the thirteenth century. The excavator, David Austin, has suggested that it was the creation of Hugh Courtenay's park that compelled their abandonment, although some of the pottery that has been found in the houses suggests that the decline of the farmsteads in the park may have been a more gradual affair: some may have continued in use later than this and been abandoned over a longer period of time.

Further Reading

Austin, D. 'Excavations in Okehampton Deer Park, Devon, 1976–8', *PDAS* 36 (1978), 191–240

Austin, D., Daggett, R.H. and Walker, M.J.C. 'Farms and Fields in Okehampton Park, Devon; The problems of Studying Medieval Landscape', *Landscape History* 2 (1980), 39–58

Austin, D. 'Dartmoor and the Upland Village of the South-West of England' in (ed.) Hooke, D. *Medieval Villages* (OUCA 5, 1985), 71–9

Barlow, F. 'Hunting in the Middle Ages', *TDA* 113 (1981), 1–11

Photograph: National Monuments Record, RCHME, 28 February 1979

Plate 62

South Hole, Hartland

South Hole lies at the south-west corner of Hartland parish, not far from Embury Beacon (plate 29). Hartland is a large parish, and the structure of its early land tenure has interesting features which have been explored by Harold Fox and Susan Pearce. King Alfred's will, dating from about 881, refers to his manor of Harton, and, following Pearse Chope, Dr Pearce has suggested that this included all the present-day parish and in addition extended south to the modern county boundary. It has been suggested that various small manors, of which South Hole was one, were granted to royal thegns out of the lands of the original royal estate. Domesday Book records the landholdings in the later eleventh century: the estates of Harton (the residual king's manor), of the minster of Hartland, and the four small manors of Welcombe (later a separate parish), Meddon, Milford and South Hole. South Hole had a chapel of its own by 1400; the site of St Heligan's lies in the rough ground upper right in the photograph.

South Hole was a self-contained hamlet in the earlier Middle Ages, and earthworks indicative of a rather larger former population can be seen in the picture. Harold Fox, working on the records of the earlier royal manor, which by the fourteenth century was in the hands of the Dynham family, has been able to demonstrate persuasively the contraction in the population of the hamlets of that part of the parish in the period 1300–1566, and it seems probable that the manor and hamlet of South Hole experienced a similar decline. Fox's research is of importance since in the past it has been suggested, by Professor Hoskins and others, that Devon hamlets represent a stable and unchanging settlement pattern. The modern understanding is that the overall picture is far more complex, representing a dynamic settlement pattern which was flexible and subject to change in response to prevailing circumstances.

Further Reading

Fox, H.S.A., 'Contraction: Desertion and Dwindling of Dispersed Settlement in a Devon Parish', *MVRG Ann. Rep.* 31 (1983), 40–2

Pearce, S.M. 'The Early Church in the Landscape: the Evidence from North Devon', *Arch. J.* 142 (1985), 255–75

Pearse Chope, R. *The Book of Hartland* (Devonshire Press, 1940)

Photograph: F.M. Griffith, Devon County Council, 22 December 1986

Plate 63

Houndtor, Manaton, Dartmoor

This photograph shows the well-known 'deserted mediaeval village' (really a hamlet) of Houndtor with unusual clarity. The light covering of snow shows the walls of the buildings standing starkly black, while masking out the variation in the vegetation on the site which usually confuses the eye in an air photograph. In the upper part of the picture the blown snow reveals slight plough-ridges on the hillside; these are believed to be the product of more recent exploitation of the area, probably at the time when many such areas of Dartmoor were brought under cultivation in the Napoleonic Wars.

The hamlet at Houndtor is a good example of a deserted site on Dartmoor. Off the moor such sites are much rarer: a declining hamlet would more often shrink down to a single farm (as, for example, Hennard Jefford, plate 113) rather than be completely abandoned. Houndtor hamlet exhibits a group of at least four farmsteads, of which the one in the foreground appears to be the most substantial. The houses are 'longhouses' (i.e. having provision for the housing of stock at their lower ends) and the farms have ancillary structures in the form of barns and lesser outbuildings. Corn-drying ovens can still be seen in some of the barns.

The hamlet was extensively excavated in the 1960s by Mrs E.M. Minter, and after her death a report on the work was published by Guy Beresford. They interpreted the site as long lived, having its origins in the Saxon period in a group of turf-built houses and continuing into the fourteenth century. More recently the settlement has been reinterpreted by David Austin and others as being of much shorter duration: perhaps a speculative incursion into the 'outfield' in response to population expansion and the climatic optimum of the twelfth to thirteenth centuries, lasting for perhaps only a few generations before its farmers retreated again to the lower land.

Further Reading

Aston, M. *Interpreting the Landscape: Landscape Archaeology in Local Studies* (Batsford, 1985)

Austin, D. 'Dartmoor and the Upland Village of the South-West of England' in (ed.) Hooke, D. *Medieval Villages* OUCA 5 (1985), 71–9

Beacham, P.M. 'The Dartmoor Longhouse', *Devon Archaeol.* 3 (1985), 23–30

Beresford, G. 'Three deserted mediaeval settlements on Dartmoor: a report on the late E. Marie Minter's excavations', *Med. Archaeol.* 23 (1979), 98–158

Linehan, C.D. 'Deserted Sites and Rabbit Warrens on Dartmoor', *Med. Archaeol.* 10 (1966), 113–44

Photograph: F.M. Griffith, Devon County Council, 17 March 1985

Plate 64

Frithelstock Priory

This photograph was taken by Professor St Joseph in 1952, at which time the layout of the priory was a little clearer than it is today. In the centre of the photograph the present parish church of Frithelstock can be seen, consisting of nave, chancel, south aisle and a tall fifteenth-century tower. The date of the foundation of the parish church is not known, but it contains Norman fragments, and may be pre-Norman in origin.

Just to the east (left) of the church is a large roofless building which actually touches its north-east corner. This is the ruined church of the Augustinian priory founded at Frithelstock in the early thirteenth century. The close proximity of the two churches is explained by the fact that, as at Hartland (the religious house from which the priory at Frithelstock was established), the prior and canons were responsible for the parish and its parishioners as well as their own religious observances. The priory, dedicated to St Gregory, was at its peak in the mid fourteenth century, when an increase to thirteen canons is recorded, but by the Dissolution there were only four.

In front of the priory church the present farmhouse, Cloister Hall, is built on the foundations of priory buildings and probably incorporates mediaeval fabric. The long range of buildings on the left side of the farm may reflect the position of the canons' dormitory range, and other elements of the priory plan may tentatively be identified. We know, however, that many buildings were pulled down quite soon after the Dissolution. Excavations by Dr Ralegh Radford in the 1930s clarified some aspects of the layout, while earthworks in the field to the east of the church probably represent other buildings, notably the Great Gate or gatehouse, which was still visible in 1794. It is clear that many traces of this small mediaeval religious establishment still survive for future archaeological study.

Further Reading

Knowles, D. and Hadcock, R.N. *Mediaeval Religious Houses* (Longman, new ed. 1972)

Pearse Chope, R. and Radford, C.A.R. 'Frithelstock Priory and Parish Church', *PDAS* 2 (1933–6), 5–27

Photograph: J.K.S. St Joseph, Cambridge University, 24 June 1952 (Crown copyright)

Plate 65

Torre Abbey

The fact that Torre Abbey was ever a religious house at all is probably rather more evident from the air than it is to the visitor approaching the site on the ground. Unlike Frithelstock, which after the Dissolution became a farmstead, Torre, in its splendid seaside situation, passed into use as a mansion. At this time the abbey was of course in a rural situation: the town of Torquay had not yet developed.

The front part of the building (that is, that side facing the golf course at the bottom of the picture) dates from the eighteenth century, but the aerial view lets us see that behind this facade the west and south ranges of the abbey cloister still exist, while the front of the building has been enlarged by the addition of two slightly projecting wings. The photograph also shows the Abbey Gatehouse, attached to the lower left angle of the main building, and, left, the mediaeval 'Spanish Barn', used before the Dissolution to store the Abbey's tithes, but reputedly named from its use as a prison for Armada sailors in 1588.

The abbey was founded in 1196 by William de Brewer as a house of Premonstratensian canons, and most of its buildings were constructed in the twelfth and thirteenth centuries. As well as the south and west ranges, seen here roofed, there was an east range (the outline of whose walls can be seen running from the right corner of the front range), while at the top of the square so formed was the abbey church. This photograph shows excavations in progress on the site of the church, carried out on behalf of Torbay Borough Council, who now maintain the abbey as a museum. Graves cut into the floor of the church are clearly visible; the excavations have also uncovered decorative mediaeval floor tiles and fragments of sculpted effigies from tombs. The church is to be laid out for display according to the results of the excavations.

Further Reading

Russell, P. *A History of Torquay and the Famous Anchorage of Torbay* (Torquay Natural History Society, 1960)

Watkin, H.R. *History of Torre Abbey* (Published by Torre Abbey, 1909)

Seymour, D. *Torre Abbey* (Published by the author, 1977)

Photograph: F.M. Griffith, Devon County Council, 16 February 1988

Plate 66

South Molton

South Molton is a town of considerable importance in the economy of north Devon, serving a large hinterland. The settlement originated in the Anglo-Saxon period or earlier, and Domesday Book appears to record a thriving community here. The Domesday survey also tells us that the manor belonged to the king, and before that to King Edward. Since South Molton is one of the Domesday Hundreds (major units of administration) of Devon it is probable that it had in fact been a royal holding since early in the Anglo-Saxon period or even before. South Molton was formally established as a borough between 1150 and 1170, when Gilbert de Turbeville introduced burgage tenure. The borough was incorporated in 1590.

One of South Molton's principal functions in the mediaeval and later periods was as a market centre, particularly for livestock. The town lies at the boundary between the fertile lowland grazing grounds of mid Devon and the uplands of Exmoor, and it played an important part in the trade in finishing and fattening stock between the two zones. However, the town was hard hit in the nineteenth century when it did not acquire a railway station until 1873, by which time railhead cattle markets had already been established at Eggesford and Molland, taking much of South Molton's trade away. The market at South Molton continues, however, to the present day.

The photograph shows the arrangement of the town around the central market square (previously known as Broad Street, and once not very 'broad', for the area now open was occupied by a network of small lanes and alleys). Below the square in the photograph the long roof of the nineteenth-century 'pannier market' is visible; just above this is the town's Guildhall. The characteristic mediaeval town plan of long narrow 'burgage plots' can be seen throughout the centre of the town: the more recent housing developments have a less tidy air.

Further Reading

Cock, J. *Records of the Antient Borough of South Molton* (1893)

Edmunds, J. *The History of South Molton* (published privately, no date, c.1986)

Photograph: F.M. Griffith, Devon County Council, 30 June 1984

Plate 67

South Zeal

This photograph shows a more modest mediaeval borough than the last. South Zeal is not even a parish in its own right, but a borough deliberately created on a virgin site within the parish of South Tawton. The probable reason for the establishment of the borough was the exploitation of the potential of the site for trade; unlike South Tawton village itself, this borough was situated directly on the line of the road between Exeter and Okehampton, offering considerable scope for wayside trading. The charter for the borough was granted in 1299: it provided for a market and two fairs. (The granting of a charter is now believed by historians sometimes to represent the formal recognition of an existing situation, rather than necessarily to provide the actual date of creation of the settlement.)

The layout of the borough reflects its *raison d'être*. The burgage plots are clearly visible, laid out at right angles to the main road: their gently curving shape suggests that they may be occupying a framework of pre-existing field strips (see also plate 83). A widening of the road in the centre of the main street shows the market place itself. Within the widened area stands the chapel of St Mary. This was originally built in the mediaeval period as a chapel of ease to save the inhabitants from having to go to the 'mother church' in South Tawton (though burials had to be conducted there), but the chapel we see now was rebuilt in 1713, and in the nineteenth century was in use as a school.

Although South Zeal today has a rather out-of-the-way feel, it was only around the end of the eighteenth century that the Okehampton road (now the A30) was diverted to pass around it on the south by the Okehampton Turnpike Trust. Before that the borough would have seen perpetual traffic along its main street. The turnpike road has now in its turn been bypassed by the modern dual carriageway of the late 1980s.

Further Reading

Beresford, M.W. *New Towns of the Middle Ages* (Lutterworth, 1967)

Timms, S.C. 'Historic Towns of Devon' in (ed.) Timms, S.C. *Archaeology of the Devon Landscape* (Devon County Council, 1980) 97–110

Roberts, B.K. *The Making of the English Village* (Longman, 1987)

Photograph: F.M. Griffith, 15 April 1984

Plates 68 and 69

The Mouth of the River Dart and Dartmouth Castle

This view is taken looking up the Dart estuary from the south-east. The town of Dartmouth is at the top of the picture, with Kingswear opposite on the near side of the river. Dartmouth Castle stands in the left foreground with Kingswear Castle at the bottom of the picture.

Dartmouth has always been a town of considerable maritime importance. With Totnes, further up the river, it played a major role in mediaeval and post-mediaeval trade, principally the export of woollen cloth and tin, and the importation of wine (but also including the smuggling of wool *out* of England), and was later, in the seventeenth and eighteenth centuries, one of the principal ports to engage in the Newfoundland fishery. The estuary itself provides a superb sheltered deep-water anchorage and, as it lies in a strategically convenient situation on the English Channel, often served in the Middle Ages as a mustering point for English fleets being assembled for foreign expeditions. Crusader fleets, for example, left from Dartmouth in 1147 and 1190. Dartmouth was, however, still vulnerable to attack from the sea, in common with the other settlements on the south Devon coast, and work on the first of Dartmouth's castles, a 'fortalice' erected above the modern Castle Point, was begun in 1388.

A further defence for the town and the harbour was the use of a chain stretched across the entrance to the estuary. In 1481 work on the construction of the present Dartmouth Castle began, followed in 1491 by that at Kingswear, and thereafter the chain ran between the two castles. The castle at Dartmouth

differs from those previously seen in this book. Rather than being the stronghold of an individual, it was built as a public defensive work, providing accommodation for a garrison but without the upper-class residential accommodation of the earlier castles. It is also noteworthy in that it was the first castle to be purpose-designed for defence by cannon. In later times the castle at Dartmouth was modified and strengthened on several occasions, but the function of Kingswear Castle was overtaken by the improved fire-power of cannon sited at Dartmouth and it ceased to have a military role. It was restored for use as a summer-house in 1855.

In more recent times, Dartmouth has been largely supplanted by Plymouth as a port for naval, passenger and mercantile traffic. The narrowness of the approach to the harbour makes it unsuited for large vessels, while the relatively poor land communications of the town prevented the success of a project earlier this century to use it as a passenger-liner terminal.

Further Reading

Freeman, R. *Dartmouth : a new History of the Port and its People* (Harbour Books, 1983)

Higham, R.A. 'Public and Private Defence in the Medieval South West: Town, Castle and Fort' in (ed.) Higham, R.A. *Security and Defence in South-West England Before 1800* (ESH 19, University of Exeter, 1987), 27–50

Martin, M. 'Changes on the Waterfront of Dartmouth, 1600-1700', *Mariners Mirror* 66 (1980), 129–36

Oppenheim, M.M. *The Maritime History of Devon* (University of Exeter, 1968)

Russell, P. *Dartmouth* (Batsford, 1950)

Saunders, A. D. *Dartmouth Castle* (HMSO Official Guide, 1983)

Watkin, H.R. *Dartmouth* (Devonshire Association Parochial Histories of Devon, 5, 1935)

Photographs: F.M. Griffith, 21 July 1983

Plate 70

Greystone Bridge, on the border between Devon and Cornwall

Greystone Bridge is one of the very few mediaeval bridges still surviving in Devon today, and one of three – Greystone, Horse and New Bridges – built to cross the Tamar in the Middle Ages. Its excellent condition testifies to the quality of its original construction, the arches and underwork being of freestone, the walls of rubble and the coping of moorstone.

The proposal to build the bridge is recorded in Bishop Lacy's Register dated 27 December 1439, where an Indulgence of forty days is granted to all penitents contributing toward its construction. The name of the bridge is not in fact a reference to its construction, even though it is made of grey stone. The Cornish manor of Greyston is recorded in documents more than a hundred years before the bridge was built, and it was from this that it took its name.

Further Reading

Henderson, C. and Coates, H. *Old Cornish Bridges* (1928, reprinted by Bradford Barton 1972)

Henderson, C. and Jervoise, E. *Old Devon Bridges* (Wheaton, 1938)

Thomas, D.L.B. 'The Bridges of Devon' in (ed.) S.C. Timms *Archaeology of the Devon Landscape* (Devon County Council, 1980), 128–37

Photograph: J.K.S. St Joseph, Cambridge University, 5 July 1953 (Crown copyright)

Plate 71

Compton Castle, Marldon

Compton Castle is a fortified manor house, but the fortifications seen here are in fact one of its latest phases. The history of this building has been researched by A.W. Everett and the Gilbert family who owned it. The earliest building on this site was probably the house of which the original Great Hall was the principal part, dating from the early fourteenth century. The present Great Hall – the tall building with steep-pitched roof running between the two side ranges in the centre of the enclosed area – is a reconstruction of this building based on architectural evidence. It is actually the most recent structure in the picture, having been built in the 1950s. At either end of the original Great Hall were service rooms.

The second main phase of building at Compton was in the later fifteenth century, when further ranges were added, and around 1520 more chambers, the five towers complete with their gunports, the 'portcullis entrance' and the curtain wall were built. It has been suggested that this phase of fortification is to be associated with the depredations of coastal pirates, but the large size of the chapel window (visible on the right-hand side of the front elevation) indicates less than a full commitment to defence, and indeed the castle is some distance from the sea.

Compton Castle was until 1800 the home of the Gilbert family whose most famous members were the sailor brothers Sir John Gilbert, who played a large part in the repulse of the Armada, and Sir Humphrey Gilbert, the explorer and founder of the Newfoundland colony. In 1930 the estate was bought back into the Gilbert family, who restored much of the fabric, and subsequently presented the property to the National Trust.

Further Reading

Compton Castle, Devon (National Trust guide leaflet, 1985)

Everett, A.W. 'The Rebuilding of the Hall at Compton Castle', *TDA* 88 (1956), 75–85

Photograph: National Monuments Record, RCHME, 9 April 1980

Plate 72

Holcombe Rogus

The front of Holcombe Court, in the centre of the picture, was described by Sir Nikolaus Pevsner as 'the most spectacular piece of Tudor domestic architecture in Devon'. The main part of this splendid house was built, on the core of the preceding mediaeval manor house, by Roger Bluett in the first half of the sixteenth century. This building was extended in the nineteenth century, the same local limestone being used for the work.

The comprehensive range of solidly built farm buildings is of course much later. The yard of the stable range, however, also includes the circular mediaeval dovecote of the old manor house. The dovecote can be seen in the centre of the photograph, on the side of the yard near the front of the house.

Holcombe Rogus church, in the foreground, is also built in the local stone, and the oldest parts of its fabric date to the thirteenth century. The influence of the Bluett family is very evident within the church: there is a rare survival of a completely enclosed family pew – the 'Court Pew' – and two large and splendid Jacobean memorials to members of the family in the north chancel chapel. Just to the left of the church in the picture the parish's 'church house' can be seen. This was originally a cross between a village hall and a pub, where the 'church ales' were held. This particular example, a fine building in itself, has recently been restored.

Behind the Court, in the parkland to the left of the picture, there appear to be traces of an earlier field system. In the field to the right of the church a series of earthwork platforms in what is now a pasture field give some indication of the extensive formal landscaping that once surrounded the great house.

Further Reading

Pevsner, N. *The Buildings of England: North Devon* (Penguin, 1952)

Gabriel, A. and Fletcher, B. *A Short History of Holcombe Rogus* (published privately, 1986)

Photograph: F.M. Griffith, Devon County Council, 11 December 1986

Plate 73

Totnes

Professor Hoskins has estimated that in 1523–5 the wealth of Totnes' inhabitants was the sixteenth greatest of all the towns in England. The town owed its mediaeval and early modern prosperity to its situation. As one of the few towns in south-east Devon at that time, sited at the lowest crossing point on the Dart, where sea-going ships could also have access, it was ideally placed to be the focus for far-ranging trading activity. Totnes had not only an extensive export trade in cloth and Dartmoor tin (largely from the stannary of Ashburton), but also a flourishing trade in goods imported from Europe and further afield. Recent excavations in the area of Fore Street – for example, on the site of the large new supermarket seen lower right in the photograph – have produced a wide range of imported sixteenth- and seventeenth-century pottery whose variety is paralleled only in the richest parts of Exeter and Plymouth. The prosperity of Totnes at this time is demonstrated by the large number of handsome sixteenth- and seventeenth-century houses still to be seen in the town, often masked by later facades.

Since those days Totnes has declined to a less spectacular prosperity. Its origins, however, are far earlier than this: there was a town here before the Norman conquest, and, as at other Saxon towns in the county, the Norman castle (top of picture) is apparently fitted into a corner of the pre-existing plan, probably overlying part of an earlier tenement layout. The stone shell-keep on top of the motte was built in the early fourteenth century. Although Totnes' town walls hardly survive physically at all (the East Gate, rebuilt in the nineteenth century, is almost the only remaining element of the town defences) their line can clearly be seen in the layout of the streets running in an oval shape around High Street. The burgage plots within the walls are built up over virtually their entire length, and at the bottom of the picture more tenements can be seen to continue outside the earlier defences, down Fore Street to the River Dart, out of frame at the bottom. These, and the tenements in the area of the Rotherfold (top left), were established in the fourteenth century to accommodate the expansion of the successful town.

In the lower right part of the formerly walled area, the parish church of St Mary can be seen. Immediately to the right of the church is the site of Totnes Priory, which was founded by Juhel, the Breton baron to whom William the Conqueror gave the town. Almost none of the priory now survives: its church lay in the open space to the east (in front) of the parish church, and its site is partly occupied by the town Guildhall, built in about 1553, which can be seen to the right of the church.

Further Reading

Laithwaite, J.M.W. 'Totnes Houses 1500–1800' in (ed.) Clark, P. *The Transformation of English Provincial Towns* (Hutchinson, 1985), 62–98

— *Totnes Buildings* (Devon Books, forthcoming 1989)

Russell, P. *The Good Town of Totnes* (Devonshire Association, 2nd ed. 1984)

Watkin, H.R. *The History of Totnes Priory and Mediaeval Town* (1914–17, 2 vols)

Photograph: F.M. Griffith, Devon County Council, 11 January 1988

Plates 74–79

Devon Villages

Professor Hoskins wrote in 1952: 'Every village in Devon was in existence by 1066, though a number of towns were not'. Some of Devon's largest modern settlements are comparatively recent: Torquay is no older than the eighteenth century, and Exmouth, now a major town and one of the fastest-growing settlements in Devon, was historically not even a parish in its own right. Until the nineteenth century its inhabitants had to go to Littleham or to Withycombe Raleigh parish churches for marriages and burials.

Many of the settlements that are thought of as villages in Devon today were really small mediaeval towns or boroughs (see pages 82-3). The latter were places that were authorized by charter specifically to function as market centres. As mentioned above (page 78), the more characteristic form of settlement in many parts of Devon was the hamlet rather than the fully fledged village; typical hamlets are illustrated in plates 62 and 63. The 'true' villages of Devon are therefore a heterogeneous group, and attempts to apply the analytical criteria used to examine this form of settlement in other parts of the country have sometimes resulted in a rather bemused response. Thus, Brian Roberts, one of the leading geographers working on the morphology of settlement types, in discussing the variety of village plans found in England, describes Bradworthy:

> If one village could occupy that focal point in the grid where all plans meet, then Bradworthy is surely a candidate; in part row village, in part agglomeration, part regular, yet part irregular, with the suggestion of both a radial structure and a grid! Close study suggests three structural parts to the plan:
>
> (i) accretions on the main green, around the church and along the roads;
>
> (ii) an irregular clustering around the smaller green; and
>
> (iii) a planned row to the north, perhaps occupying the ends of former arable strips (Hoskins and Finberg, 1952, 290-1; 312-3).
>
> Three questions are fundamental; was the mediaeval church and its yard added to an existing nucleus; is the row a secondary feature; what part of the visible plan represents the original nucleus? These are, of course, questions to carry into the field, for no map reveals the character of the boundaries and slopes or the presence of earthwork remains.
>
> (Roberts, 1987, p.68)

Plate 74 Bradworthy *Photograph: F.M. Griffith, Devon County Council, 7 July 1984*

This passage has been quoted at length, since it illustrates the methods of the modern researcher into village plans. Perhaps the majority of Devon villages do not pose quite so many problems: the overriding factor that has controlled the development of many of our villages has been topographical – the village, once established in a certain spot, has had to grow as its physical position permitted. Clovelly (plate 75) on the north coast of the Hartland peninsula, is a prime example of this dominant factor: the initial siting of the village must have depended on the presence of a beach where boats could land (later improved by the construction of a small harbour), and subsequent development could only grow up the steep combe stretching inland from the sea. Stokeinteignhead (plate 77) is another village whose development appears to have been principally conditioned by its siting at the junction of several small valleys, up which the growing settlement expanded. Membury, too, seems to straggle away up the valley from the parish church (plate 76).

At Ugborough in the South Hams (plate 78), on the other hand, the village may well have at its core an earlier hilltop enclosure, though the pattern of lanes radiating regularly out from its central square are suggestive of a planned origin. Professor Hoskins described Ugborough as a typical 'compact village', which he regarded as an uncharacteristic feature in Devon. Northlew, north of Okehampton, does not have its position dictated by a hilltop siting in the same way, but here too the structure of the village is dominated by the church and the very large square (plate 79).

Much work remains to be done in the study of Devon villages, as in so many aspects of the history of rural settlement (see also p.124). As Roberts has

suggested, only an approach combining detailed analytical work on the ground with the use of all available documentary sources is likely to permit us to make a more sophisticated study of these problems.

Further Reading

Hoskins, W.G. 'The Making of the Agrarian Landscape' in Hoskins, W.G. and Finberg, H.P.R. *Devonshire Studies* (Cape, 1952), 289–333

Roberts, B.K. *The Making of the English Village* (Longman, 1987)

Rowley, T. *Villages in the Landscape* (Dent, 1978)

Taylor, C. *Village and Farmstead* (G. Phillip, 1983)

Plate 75 Clovelly *Photograph: F.M. Griffith, 14 August 1983*

Plate 76 Membury *Photograph: F.M. Griffith, Devon County Council, December 1986*

Plate 77 Stokeinteignhead

ograph: F.M. Griffith, Devon County Council, 18 July 1985

Plate 78 Ugborough *Photograph: F.M. Griffith, Devon County Council, 13 July 1984*

Plate 79 Northlew *Photograph: F.M. Griffith, Devon County Council, 14 August 1987*

Plate 80

Plymouth Citadel

The earliest fortification known on Plymouth Hoe is recorded on a plan from the time of Henry VIII, which shows a massive square tower with cannon on the point at the eastern end of the Hoe, from which a wall runs westward along the sea front to a second tower. No trace of these defences now survives, and they seem not to have been maintained in good order for very long. The events of 1588, when the Spanish Armada might have sacked the town, engendered a new concern in Plymouth for its security; in 1592–6 a new fort was therefore constructed.

The Royal Citadel as we see it today is predominantly the fortification designed by Sir Bernard de Gomme for Charles II in 1665, which incorporated some of the remains of the preceding late-sixteenth-century fort. The geometry of the ramparts and bastions of the new fortification represented the finest military science of the time.

In the lower right corner of the photograph, above the little harbour, an artillery platform at a lower level than the rest of the defences can be seen. This was part of the original design, built to protect the Cattewater from attack from the sea, and remodelled in the 1750s to provide cover for the Dockyard. Cannon of the day were capable of firing only at a limited angle below the horizontal, and thus guns for attacking sea-level targets could not be sited on top of the Hoe but had to be set on this firing platform and in bastions in the Lower Fort (bottom right). The picture also shows the shoreline outworks, predominantly constructed in the later eighteenth century, and the military buildings within the Citadel: barracks, workshops and stores, and administration buildings. These represent survivals from a number of different phases of the Royal Citadel's use, ranging from some of de Gomme's original structures to a major rebuilding of the barrack accommodation around 1900.

The Citadel is at present occupied by 29 Commando Regiment, Royal Artillery.

Further Reading

Woodward, F.W. *Citadel, A History of the Royal Citadel, Plymouth* (Devon Books, 1987)

— 'The Royal Citadel, Plymouth', *Devon Archaeol.* 2 (1984), 9-12

Photograph: F.M. Griffith, Devon County Council, 16 February 1988

Plate 81

Braunton Great Field

The Great Field at Braunton, to the north of the Taw – Torridge estuary, is an exceptional survival of the once widespread system of cultivating large common fields in strips with no permanent divisions. In the Middle Ages the occupancy of the strips was divided among a group of tenants to ensure an equable division of good and poor land: now the strips at Braunton belong permanently to a smaller number of farmers who still cultivate parts of the field in the traditional narrow strips. As recently as 1840, however, the Tithe Map recorded some 600 strips in the hands of as many as sixty cultivators.

It was once thought that because of the scarcity of any obvious evidence for open-field cultivation in Devon it had never formed a normal part of the agricultural economy here, the Great Field being some sort of recent agricultural anomaly. More recent work, in particular by Professor Finberg, has demonstrated that open, or divided, fields were previously common in Devon, but that in most parts of the county the practice of open-field cultivation was superseded during the Middle Ages, and did not survive into the eighteenth and nineteenth centuries as it did in the Midland counties. Finberg observed that the Braunton open field was referred to in a document of 1324, which recorded a particular holding of 26½ acres in twenty-five separate parcels or strips. The very names of some of the fourteenth-century divisions of the field can still be recognized today.

Comparison of aerial photographs with the Ordnance Survey plan will show the continuity of the land divisions here, even though they are marked only by low grassed baulks or 'landsherds' between the strips and sometimes by large beach pebbles at the ends of the strips. Although the overall area of the field system has been much reduced, and consolidation of holdings has taken place with the reduction in the total number of farmers, sufficient single strips are still visible to give a most striking impression of the former regime. Today the Great Field is one of the few surviving examples of open-field cultivation in the whole of Britain, and as such is of national importance.

Beyond the Great Field itself lies Braunton Marsh: a major piece of land reclamation from salt-marsh undertaken in the nineteenth century. The marshes have a particularly good range of nineteenth-century farm buildings scattered about in isolated positions in the fields. Further still, beyond the marshes, a complex sand-dune system, now a nature reserve, lies between the reclaimed land and the Atlantic.

Further Reading

Devon County Council *Braunton Great Field and Marshes: a Countryside Study (1982)*

Finberg, H.P.R. 'The Open Field in Devon' in Hoskins, W.G. and Finberg, H.P.R. *Devonshire Studies* (Cape, 1952), 265–88

Fox, H.S.A. 'Field Systems of East and South Devon: Part 1 East Devon', *TDA* 104 (1972), 81–136

Slee, A.H. 'The Open Fields of Braunton', *TDA* 84 (1952), 142–9

Photograph: F.M. Griffith, Devon County Council, 18 December 1985

Plate 82

Strip Fields at Challacombe, Dartmoor

This photograph of Challacombe Down was taken looking west from a point just south of Grimspound (plate 21). At the top of the picture runs the Moretonhampstead–Princetown road, and to this side of it the important nineteenth-century mines of Golden Dagger and Birch Tor and Vitifer (plate 88) can be seen. The dark patch to the left of the picture is Soussons Plantation.

Snow lying on the hillside shows up a number of low banks defining strips. These mostly lie parallel with the contours, but on the southern flank, where the slope is less steep, they run up the hill. These lynchets are the edges of strip fields farmed from the hamlet of Challacombe, seen in the centre of the picture. Challacombe is now a single farm, but in the Middle Ages it was a hamlet of some twelve buildings: the remains of several of the longhouses still survive. Each of the strips was separately farmed and we know from a seventeenth-century map that each farmer held strips throughout the field system, as was the case at Braunton. The fields at Challacombe are no longer cultivated and are now used for grazing. The lynchets can still be clearly seen on the ground, and in early summer are spectacularly outlined by bluebells.

Further Reading

Bonney, D. J. 'Former Farms and Fields at Challacombe, Manaton, Dartmoor' in (eds) Gregory, K.J. and Ravenhill, W. *Exeter Essays in Geography* (University of Exeter, 1971), 83–91

Photograph: F.M. Griffith, Devon County Council, 17 March 1985

Plate 83

Combe Martin

Although this photograph of Combe Martin, on the north Devon coast, was taken in 1948 the appearance of the village has not changed greatly since then. The village is strung out for over 2 km along one main street which runs down to the sea, through the combe which gives the place its name. In Domesday Book the manor is just called *Comba* – the Martin came later, probably from the name of a twelfth-century holder of the manor. Much of the past wealth of the area has come from silver and lead mines on both sides of the valley; these were exploited from the thirteenth century intermittently down to the middle of the nineteenth, and extensive traces of the mines survive around the combe.

A striking feature of this photograph is the great number of small strip fields running up from the bottom of the valley on either side. These fields probably have their origin in a system of common fields like those at Braunton and Challacombe (see previous pages), but they have evolved in a different way. Whereas in other parts of Devon when the open fields ceased to be held in common they were consolidated into more compact holdings by mutual exchange and were enclosed as more or less rectangular fields, here apparently the strips passed into separate tenure unconsolidated, so that many of the old strips were fossilized just as they were. Traces of a similar phenomenon can be seen in the small patches of relict field strips in many other parts of the county, both surviving on the ground and recorded on the modern map and, more clearly, in the landholdings recorded in the Tithe Maps of the period around 1840. This is the evidence that allows us to assert that open fields were once common in Devon (see above under Braunton), but now Combe Martin certainly provides the most spectacular surviving example of 'fossilized' strips in the county.

At the end of the last century the little fields were intensively used, and indeed famous, for the cultivation of strawberries, which were then transported far afield by sea and by the railway in existence at that time.

Photograph: J.K.S. St Joseph, Cambridge University, 29 June 1948

Further Reading

Fox, H.S.A. 'Field Systems of East and South Devon: Part 1 East Devon', *TDA* 104 (1972), 81–136

Plate 84

Mediaeval and modern fields at Stockland

Stockland lies in the north-east of Devon. Historically the parish was a detached portion of the county of Dorset, and it was not included in Devon until 1832. Here we see a pattern of fields which contrasts strongly with that in the preceding photographs: this is a landscape of which different parts have reached their present appearance at widely different times.

We know from recent fieldwork in this area by Nan Pearce that the valleys of Stockland and Membury were extensively exploited in the Mesolithic period, but the oldest manmade features visible in the landscape here are the two enclosures known as Stockland Great Camp and Stockland Little Camp, both of which are believed to date from the first millennium B.C. The Little Camp is the circular enclosure on the right-hand side of the picture; the Great Camp is the irregular-shaped enclosure upper left with high bushy hedges. Like many such sites in Devon, these are not securely dated, but the Great Camp in particular has a number of the features of a typical hilltop defended site of the Iron Age. Apart from these two enclosures, a number of other circular fields suggest other early elements in the landscape.

The foreground of the picture shows a pattern of rather irregular fields that appear to have accreted around these earliest features – a fairly typical Devon fieldscape. By contrast, the upper part of the picture shows fields with markedly straight hedges and very few hedgerow trees. This is one of the few parts of Devon where we can see a classic 'enclosure landscape': the whole of this part of the picture was open heath until it was made into fields by Parliamentary Enclosure in 1864. As was mentioned above (under Braunton), Parliamentary Enclosure is a rare phenomenon in Devon, as most of the open fields seem to have been enclosed by mutual arrangement before the end of the mediaeval period. This part of Devon was one of the last areas where Parliamentary Enclosure took place; Beacon Hill, Upottery, just north of here, was enclosed in 1874 by means of the last Enclosure Award in the county.

Further Reading

Berridge, P.J. 'Mesolithic Sites in the Yarty Valley', *PDAS* 43 (1985), 1–22

Hoskins, W.G. 'The Making of the Agrarian Landscape' in Hoskins, W.G. and Finberg, H.P.R. *Devonshire Studies* (Cape, 1952) 289–333

Taylor, C.C. *Fields in the English Landscape* (Dent, 1975)

Turner, M. *English Parliamentary Enclosure: Its Historical Geography and Economic History* (1980)

Photograph: F.M. Griffith, Devon County Council, 21 March 1988

Plate 85

Sourton Down

This photograph shows another field system of a different type. The light covering of snow has revealed features which in normal conditions are quite difficult to make out on the ground: the low ridges of a narrow-rig cultivation system. It is probable that this dates from the later eighteenth century, when quite extensive areas of poorly drained upland such as this were being brought into short-term cultivation.

Lying within this field system, and apparently pre-dating it, a sub-square feature composed of concentric banks and ditches shows up clearly in the snow. This earthwork has proved very puzzling to archaeologists, and has been variously identified as a Bronze Age barrow, a Roman signal station and a small redoubt or battery of the English Civil War. These features on Sourton Down lie very close to the line of the new Okehampton bypass, which has in fact destroyed a substantial part of the field system; during limited rescue excavations carried out in the area by the Central Excavation Unit a small trench was cut in the earthwork (which is a Scheduled Ancient Monument). Unfortunately this enigmatic structure failed to deliver any positive dating evidence in the excavation and its date and purpose remain uncertain, although informed opinion is currently tending toward the Civil War explanation, in view of the known engagement on Sourton Down and the site's position commanding the top of the Down. One problem for the archaeologist is that a situation that is strategically useful in one age is likely also to be so in others; thus the site of a Roman signal station is often found to be one desirable for modern communications equipment.

Further Reading

Balkwill, C.J. and Silvester, R.J. 'Earthworks on Sourton Down, near Okehampton', *PDAS* 34 (1976), 86–9

Kerr, J.B. 'Excavations in advance of the A30 Okehampton Bypass, Devon', *PDAS* forthcoming

Photograph: F.M. Griffith, Devon County Council, 17 March 1985

Plate 86

Exeter Canal Basin and Quay

This photograph, taken in 1985, shows the view looking up the River Exe from the south-east. Exeter Cathedral is in the top right-hand corner and the Exe Bridges roundabout can be seen top left. The photograph shows the areas of Exeter that were important to its commercial success in the mediaeval and early modern periods, in the heyday of the Exeter woollen trade. Where the river bends to the left in the picture, the Custom House, built by the City Chamber (the forerunner of the City Council) in 1680, can be seen straight ahead.

Recent documentary research and excavations by Exeter Museums Archaeological Field Unit have demonstrated that at the time the Custom House was built the line of the quay was further back than its present position: excavations in the Quay House (the long building with a white end wall to the right of the Custom House) have proved the building to be a large seventeenth-century warehouse. Excavations in front of the building identified the wall of the covered dock which lay next to the warehouse. The Quay House has been preserved, and part serves as an Interpretation Centre for visitors. Just in front of the Quay House in the picture the tall stone warehouses built in 1835 can be seen. These never played quite such a key role in the city's trade as was expected, for the coming of the railway in 1844 took trade away from the canal and quay almost immediately.

The basin at the head of the canal can be seen to the left of the river. The canal itself was the first in Britain to be built with pound locks. It was opened in 1566 to permit goods to be brought by water up the estuary to Exeter, bypassing the weir at Countess Wear and also the shallows of the river. The canal was a persistent cause of concern to the City, and the Chamber Act Books record continuing litigation, engineering problems and frequent silting-up. The entrance to the canal is just out of the picture where the river widens on the left. The boats originally passed out of the canal into the river to dock at the quay, but in 1830 the canal basin was opened. The period of full operation for the basin, too, was affected by the arrival of the railway, though eventually a branch line was put through to it. The canal, however, continued to be used commercially on a small scale until the recent past: in the early 1970s it saw regular cargoes of timber and fuel oil. The basin itself is now used for private boats and by Exeter Maritime Museum.

Since this photograph was taken the view from this point has been transformed by the construction of a suspension bridge for foot traffic over the river at the bend in the picture. At the time of writing a number of housing developments are proposed on either side of the river in this area, which will further change the appearance of this historically important part of Exeter.

Further Reading

Clark, E.A.G. *The Ports of the Exe Estuary 1660-1860* (University of Exeter, 1960)

Clew, K.R. *The Exeter Canal* (Phillimore, 1984)

Henderson, C.G. 'The Archaeology of Exeter Quay', *Devon Archaeol.* 4 (forthcoming)

— 'Exeter Quay in the 16th and 17th Centuries', *Maritime South West* 4 (1988)

Hoskins, W.G. *Industry, Trade and People in Exeter 1688–1800* (University of Exeter, 2nd ed. 1968)

Photograph: F.M. Griffith, Devon County Council, 6 March 1986

Plates 87–89

The Dartmoor Tin Industry

The mineral wealth of Dartmoor, particularly its tin, has been exploited for many centuries, and quite probably from prehistoric times, though this has never been proved beyond doubt. From the air it is possible fully to appreciate the extent of the impact which exploitation of the tin deposits has had upon the Dartmoor landscape. The extraction of tin from the moor can be divided into three main categories: streamworking, open working, and underground mining. No attempt will be made here to detail the industrial processes involved: in recent years a considerable amount of research has been undertaken on this topic, and a selection of relevant publications is given below.

Streamworking entails the use of running water to separate out tin-bearing stones from surface alluvial deposits. Modern fieldwork has done much to elucidate the exact methods of the tin-streamers, and, laborious though streamworking was in the amount of sheer person-power required to turn over the tin-ground by shovel, this technique was in use up to the last century. The characteristic field remains of streamworking are the series of parallel, usually curving, banks of upcast left as the tinners worked systematically across the surface of the ground. These can be seen in plate 87, at Swincombe Head. The spoilheaps can often be seen running roughly parallel with the existing course of a stream. The bed of the stream and the surrounding deposits were worked for the alluvial deposits of tin, while the stream itself supplied water both to provide power and to wash the excavated tin-bearing material to separate out the tin. Where a stream had formed a valley it also provided a point of access into tin-lodes in the surrounding hillsides. Close observation will often show the course of the stream to have been significantly altered by the tinners as they used it to work the deposits.

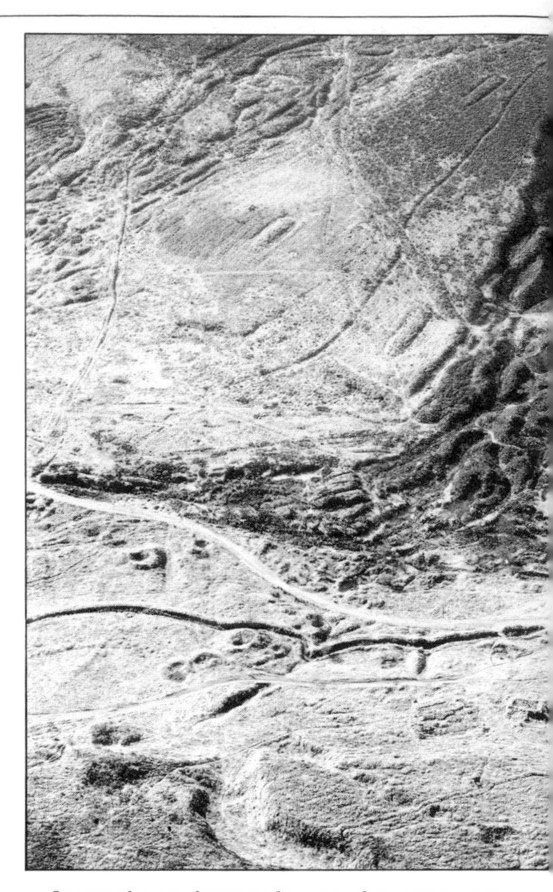

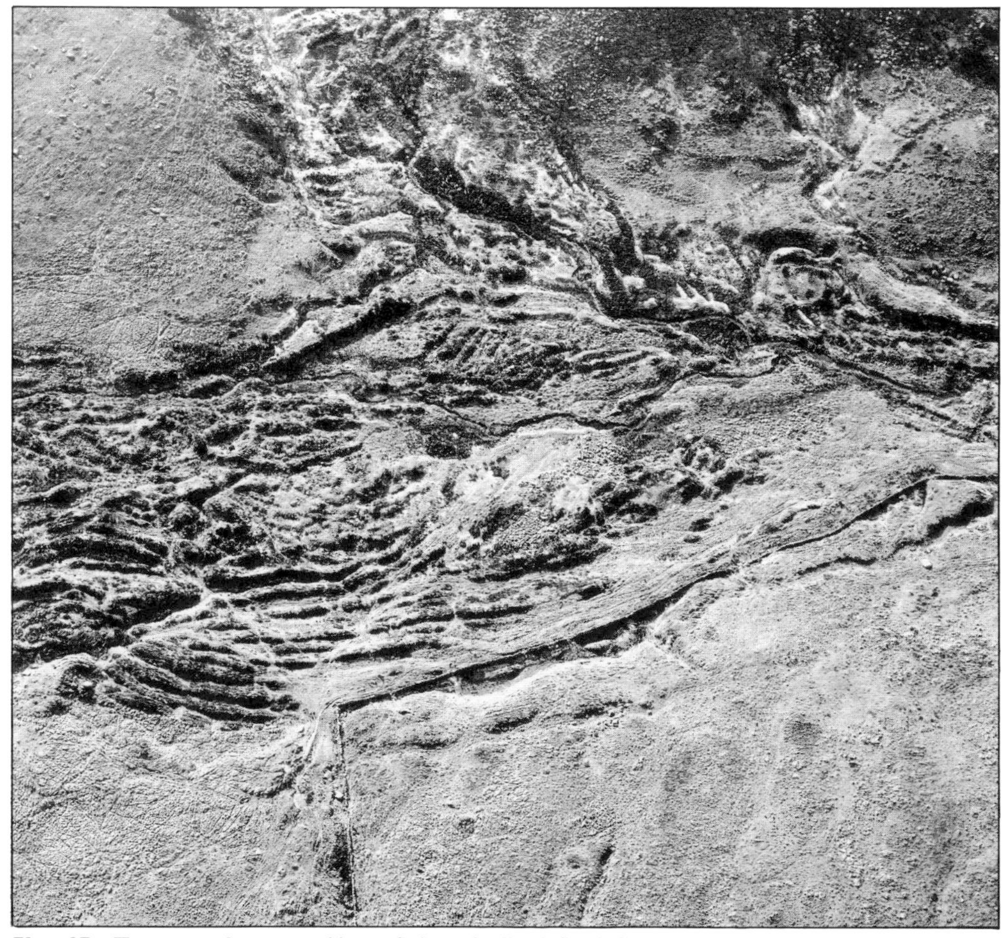

Plate 87 The traces of streamworking at Swincombe Head, South Dartmoor.

Openworks or beamworks are the great open trenches visible in plate 88: this results from digging down from the surface to follow a tin-bearing lode for so long as it was economic to remove the overburden. Openworks are often associated with lines of trial pits, which can be seen in plate 89, at the right-hand side: these were dug to trace the course of the lode and to assess its quality.

From the air, the traces of true underground mining on Dartmoor are probably the least apparent, though in the nineteenth-century mining boom this was the predominant method of extraction. Often mines are associated with areas of openworking: the tin was extracted by opencast methods for as long as practicable and thereafter, sometimes much later, the deeper deposits could be exploited by mining. The most obvious traces of true mining are the mine spoilheaps and the wheelpits of the enormous waterwheels used at some mines for drainage.

As well as the evidence for the primary extraction of tin-bearing deposits, copious field remains of features associated with subsequent processing may be seen. Buddles or settling pits, used to separate the tin stone from the other crushed stone, often survive, as do remains of the stamping mills (for crushing the stone) and blowing houses (for smelting the tin).

Plate 88 Streamworking (upper left), openworks (top centre), leats (centre right), trial pits (centre), and the buildings of Birch Tor and Vitifer Mine, North Bovey, one of the last mines to operate on Dartmoor. Photographs of the mine in operation are published by Tom Greeves in *Tin Mines and Miners of Dartmoor.* The long subrectangular mounds on the opposite hillside are 'pillow mounds': artificial mounds for rabbits to live in. These were an important part of the Dartmoor economy from the mediaeval period onwards, used both on a commercial scale and in small numbers, particularly by the tinners, to supplement the diet.

Plate 89 Mineshafts and trial pits at Whiteworks Mine, Hexworthy. The mining complex is intermingled with the fields of a farm. The curious appearance of some of the shafts is the result of stone walls having been built around them to keep out the stock of the farm which succeeded the mine on this site. In the bottom left-hand corner of the photograph the Devonport Leat can be seen running southward to Plymouth.

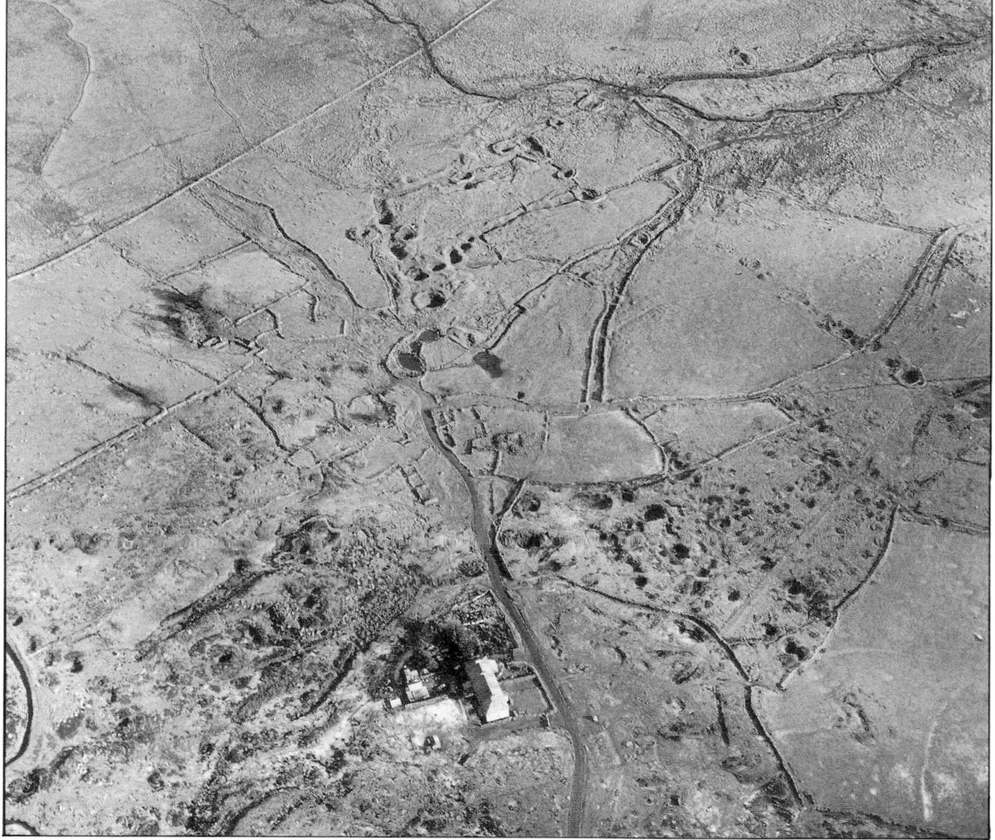

Photographs: F.M. Griffith, Devon County Council, 21 January 1988

These processes were frequently carried out very close to the source of the tin, and evidence for them is often found amidst the remains of the extractive process itself. Leats (artificial water channels) were cut across the moor, sometimes for great distances, to power water-wheels which drove crushing and drainage machinery, and to work the bellows for the smelting furnace.

Further Reading

Broughton, D.G. 'The Birch Tor and Vitifer tin mining complex', *Trans. Corn. Inst. Engineers* 24 (1968/9), 25–49

Burt, R. *et al. Devon and Somerset Mines* (University of Exeter, 1984)

Gerrard, S. 'Streamworking in medieval Cornwall', *J. Trevithick Soc.* 14 (1987), 7–31

Greeves, T. 'A History of Whiteworks Tin Mine, Part 1: 1790 to 1848', *PMMCJ* 11 no. 2 (1980), 11–17

—— 'The Archaeological Potential of the Devon Tin Industry' in (ed.) Crossley, D.W. *Medieval Industry* (CBA Res. Rep. 40, 1981), 85–95

—— 'The Dartmoor Tin Industry – a simple guide to the field remains', *Devon Archaeol.* 3 (1985), 31–41

—— *Tin Mines and Miners of Dartmoor* (Devon Books, 1986)

Hamilton Jenkin, A.K. *Mines of Devon vol 1: the Southern Area* (David & Charles, 1974)

Newman, P. 'The Moorland Meavy – a Tinners' Landscape', *TDA* 114 (1987), 223–40

Penhallurick, R.D. *Tin in Antiquity* (Institute of Metals, 1986)

Plate 90

Agricultural Earthworks north of Tiverton

As described in the Introduction, the low angle of winter sunlight can often show up quite slight earthworks with great clarity. In this photograph a number of different features can be seen standing out. Probably the most immediately apparent are the series of little channels or 'gutters' running around the curve of the hillside. They are particularly clear in the foreground, but traces of ploughed-out ones can be seen on the far side of the dip in the field. The rough ground in the dip marks the course of the flow from a spring, and the channels have been used to carry water around the contours from the spring to the whole field. The water, controlled by gates and sluices, overflowed from the gutters and trickled down over the surface of the grass. This is a permanent pasture field, and the device of gutters, also sometimes described as a catchwork meadow or watermeadow (though this last refers more properly to a flat system of irrigation), was an innovation developed in the West Country, designed to warm and nourish the grass to bring it on earlier. This invention, though attributed to the 'Agricultural Revolution', in fact preceded the main phase of agricultural mechanization in the east of England which has usually been considered the starting point of agricultural improvement. In this example, photographed at Palfreys Barton, north of Tiverton, the nutritional content of the liquid is much enhanced by the provision of a slurry pit at the top of the system, just above the stone wall of the lane, which fed manure from the farmstead into the system of gutters. The organized distribution of slurry on the land is nothing new.

In the centre left of the picture a series of low ridges can be seen running up the slope. This is not 'ridge and furrow', though it is sometimes mistaken for it: the ridges are the remains of an orchard. They were made in order to improve the drainage, and in this case the mounds that surrounded the individual trees can also be seen. We know that this particular orchard was taken out before 1915, but as no other disturbance of the ground has since taken place, the earthworks still look quite fresh.

Along the top of the field by the wall a series of earthworks can be seen. The platform near the existing house is the site of a building that lasted into this century, but the reason for the earthwork platform within a banked rectilinear enclosure opposite the big barn is lost from memory. It may well represent the site of a separate farmstead in existence at a time when a complete hamlet stood here.

Further Reading

Kerridge, E. *The Agricultural Revolution* (Allen & Unwin, 1967), 251–68 : Chapter VI 'Floating the Watermeadows'

Vancouver, C. *General View of the Agriculture of the County of Devon* (1808, reissued by David & Charles, 1969) : Chapter VIII 'Grass Land'

Photograph: F.M. Griffith, Devon County Council, 11 December 1986

Plate 91

Tiverton from the east

This photograph shows how the textile industry is still a dominant feature of the appearance of Tiverton. On the far side of the River Exe the present Heathcoat's factory can be seen, its riverside siting dating from the time when, like all the textile industry, it relied on water for its power; the leat that served the earlier mills can be seen cutting across the bend in the river. Tiverton has played an important role in the Devon cloth industry since the late fifteenth century, and the names of such prominent merchants as John Greenway and Peter Blundell are still remembered today. The pre-eminence of Devon in the woollen trade faded in the late eighteenth century and it was into this situation of relative decline that John Heathcoat came from the Midlands in 1816, to take over one of the mills to make lace. The factory we see today replaced the old one, burned down in 1936.

Beyond the factory in the photograph, in the area known as West Exe, orderly rows of workers' and artisans' housing can be seen. In Devon, with its relatively small-scale industries, purpose-built workers' housing is a rare phenomenon in comparison with the Midlands and the North. The houses seen here date from the nineteenth century, but the first record of the suburb of West Exe is as early as 1504.

On the nearer side of the river the old centre of Tiverton can be seen (left centre), the market buildings prominent, though many of the old lanes have now disappeared from this area. Tiverton Castle can be seen near the bend in the river, with the parish church of St Peter beyond it.

At the bottom right of the picture lies a newly constructed supermarket illustrating vividly the different scale of modern development.

Further Reading

Allen, W.G. *John Heathcoat and His Heritage* (Christopher Johnson, 1958)

Dunsford, M. *Historical Memoirs of the Town and Parish of Tiverton* (1790)

Field, J.J. 'Excavations in St Andrews Street and West Exe, Tiverton', *PDAS* 35 (1977), 63–79

Snell, F. J. *The Chronicles of Twyford* (1892)

Youings, J. 'King James' Charter to Tiverton, 1615', *TDA* 99 (1967), 147–63

Photograph: F.M. Griffith, Devon County Council, 10 July 1985

Plate 92

Shobrooke Church and Barton

Shobrooke lies in the heart of 'red Devon' between Tiverton and Crediton. This is one of the parts of Devon where recent aerial reconnaissance has been successful in identifying the remains of numerous settlement sites of probable prehistoric date: the richness of the soil here has meant that the land has been regularly cultivated for many generations, removing most above-ground traces of the sites.

Like many Devon parishes, Shobrooke has no village (see p. 66): here only the church and the barton stand together. The church, St Swithin's, is a handsome stone building. It has a somewhat dominant Victorian south aisle, built by Edward Ashworth, but the oldest part of the church, the doorway, dates from the mid twelfth century. The aerial view often provides an interesting angle on a church: in this photograph the stair turret of the square tower can be seen standing out.

Across the road from the church stands Shobrooke Barton (bottom of picture). This is a fairly typical large mid-Devon farmhouse of cob on stone footings, with a massive lateral chimney stack of the local 'trap' – volcanic stone from the Thorverton area – against the road. The house dates back at least to the seventeenth century and almost certainly earlier.

Above the barton in the photograph is an impressive quadrilateral of farm buildings, a very fine farmyard. On the short side of the farmyard, nearest the barton, are two barns, separately built during the late eighteenth or early nineteenth century, and a granary stands at the angle nearest the church, but the other three sides of the yard are formed by a contemporary group of three long ranges of linhays – two-storey open-fronted buildings with stock accommodation beneath and haylofts above. These are built of cob on stone footings, with upper floors supported on pine posts. At some point the whole establishment seems to have been used for the large-scale raising of yarded cattle, whether or not this was the original purpose of the farmyard.

Photograph: F.M. Griffith, Devon County Council, 10 March 1988

Plate 93

Haytor Quarry and Tramway

Quarrying of granite on Dartmoor is a recent phenomenon. Most of the stone used in buildings around the moor and in the manufacture of such items as millstones, cider pounds and troughs is moorstone, which is stone taken from the surface of the moor. It was not until the end of the eighteenth century that quarrying for granite began. It soon achieved considerable economic importance. Haytor Quarry is a dramatic illustration of the link between quarrying and transportation: the success of the quarry, high on the side of Haytor Down, was dependent upon the construction of a tramway to remove the products of the quarry from the moor to a canal that served to carry the granite down to the sea for shipping.

The quarry, tramway and canal started work around 1820. They were developed by George Templer of Stover, Teigngrace. It soon became a successful concern, and provided some of the stone for London Bridge (the bridge that went to America) and the British Museum. The last use of Haytor granite was in 1919, when the quarries provided the stone for the Exeter war memorial.

The quarries themselves and parts of the tramway and the Stover canal are still visible today on the ground, and the lines of the tracks of the tramway can clearly be seen on the photograph. The most striking feature of the tramway is its construction: the 'rails' are made from the granite that they were to carry.

The photograph also shows prehistoric enclosures, hut circles, and fields. At the bottom is an area of mediaeval tin streamworking.

Further Reading

Crossing, W. *The Dartmoor Worker* (David & Charles, new ed. 1966)

Devon County Council *Haytor Granite Tramway and Stover Canal Countryside Study* (1986)

Ewans, M.C. *The Haytor Granite Tramway and Stover Canal* (David & Charles, 1977)

Harris, H. *The Industrial Archaeology of Dartmoor* (David & Charles, 1968, rev. ed. 1987)

Photograph: National Monuments Record, RCHME, 19 April 1982

Plate 94

Powder Mills, Lydford

'Powder Mills', near Cherrybrook in Lydford parish, means exactly what it says. This is a place where gunpowder was manufactured. The location, right out in the middle of the moor, was deliberately chosen because of the hazardous nature of the operations. Gunpowder was a commodity in increasing demand for use in the quarrying and other industries in the mid nineteenth century, and this manufactory was established in 1844 to supply both Devon and Cornish mines and quarries.

An air view is a good way to appreciate the layout of this establishment, since the buildings are well spread out to minimize the risk of one explosion setting off others. On the right-hand side of the picture three pairs of the mills themselves can be seen: the now roofless buildings linked by a curving leat bringing water from the East Dart River. The central wheelpit of each pair is visible: this provided the power for the stones grinding up the mixture of charcoal, saltpetre and sulphur which made up the gunpowder. Other buildings equipped with water-wheels to drive machinery lie among the trees on the left of the picture, and the building at the lower right, whose flue and chimney can be seen, is probably a stoving house for drying the finished product.

Beyond the range of the photograph, to the left, nearer to the Moretonhampstead road and well out of blast range, the remains of workers' housing, a cooperage (to make barrels for the gunpowder) and other buildings relating to the mills can still be seen on the ground. In their heyday the mills employed up to a hundred people, but the invention of dynamite ultimately finished the market for gunpowder, and the works shut down in 1899.

Further Reading

Crocker, G. *The Gunpowder Industry* (Shire Album 160, 1986)

Harris, H. *The Industrial Archaeology of Dartmoor* (David & Charles, 1968, rev. ed. 1987)

Photograph: F.M. Griffith, Devon County Council, 22 December 1986

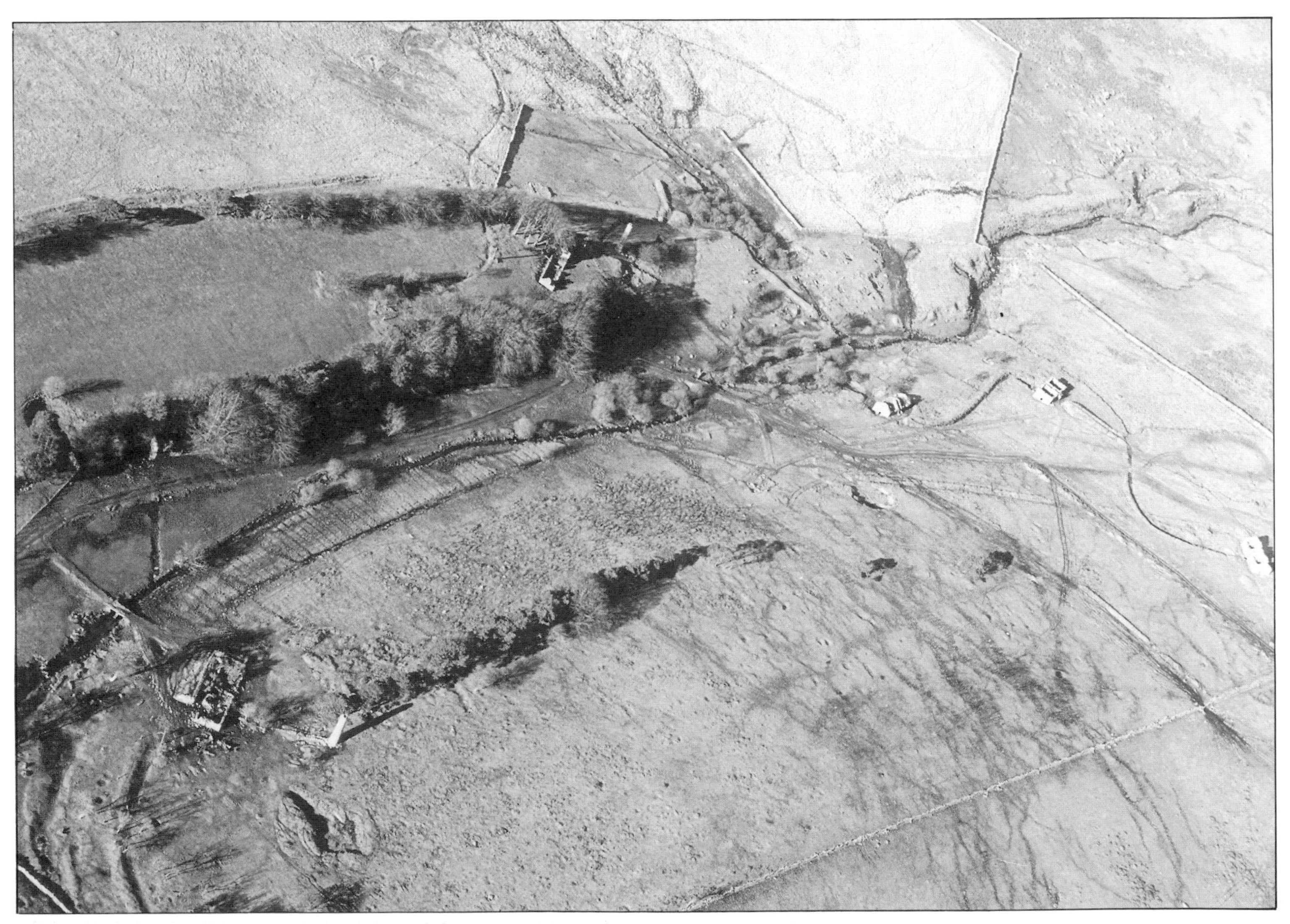

Plate 95

Canal at Bude

Bude is not in Devon but in Cornwall. The town is situated on the north Cornish coast, a few miles south of the county boundary and of Embury Beacon (page 29). Because of the parlous state of road transport in Devon until at least the eighteenth century, access into north-west Devon was easier from the sea than across the county by land. The transport of heavy goods into the agricultural hinterland was always a problem, and one which increased after the introduction of more intensive methods of farming in the eighteenth century, which required the carriage inland of large volumes of lime and sea-sand (much of it from Bude itself) for fertilizer. This was the problem the Bude Canal, seen here, was designed to solve, and in comparison with some canals of its day it solved it very successfully. Built in 1819–23, it had two branches which ran one to Holsworthy and the other to Launceston. In addition it had a branch to the reservoir at Tamar Lake, which was constructed in order to store water for the canal and only started to serve as a public-service water-supply reservoir after the canal had ceased working. The canal was in its day the longest tub-boat canal in England, and that with the greatest number of inclined planes (slopes between two levels of canal over which boats were hauled by mechanical means). The canal flourished in its early years but later declined as other forms of transport improved. The arrival of the railway in Bude in 1898 finally killed it: all heavy goods could now be carried by an inherently more flexible system, which connected with the main rail networks. (The railway itself has of course now left Bude.)

The photograph is taken looking into Bude Haven from the west. Though Bude had always had some kind of a harbour, it was described by Borlase in 1754 as 'a sandy creek for small vessels'. The harbour seen here (at low water) is essentially that built in 1818–23 to accommodate ships offloading cargoes for the tub-boats. Two watercourses are seen entering the harbour: that on the left is the River Neet, and that on the right the canal, with a sea-lock 35 m long at its entrance. The breakwater, to the left of the canal entrance, was an important factor in the success of the whole project. The present one was built in 1838–43 to replace the original, smaller, one which was destroyed in a storm in 1838.

Further Reading

Bere, R. and Stamp, B.D. *The Book of Bude and Stratton* (Barracuda, 1980)

Hadfield, C. *The Canals of South West England* (David & Charles, 1967)

Harris, H. and Ellis, M. *The Bude Canal* (David & Charles, 1972)

Photograph: F.M. Griffith, Devon County Council, 23 August 1985

Plate 96

The Teign Estuary

This photograph shows some of the fertile lowland country of south-east Devon where in recent years large numbers of settlement sites, many of them probably dating from the first millennium B.C. have been identified by aerial photography (e.g. plate 47). Looking up the estuary through this land, the mass of Dartmoor can be seen rising in the background. Between the moor and the estuary lies the Bovey Basin, an area whose ball-clay deposits have been mined since the late seventeenth century. The products of this industry were brought down the river in barges and shipped from Teignmouth, as was the granite from Haytor (plate 93).

At the bottom of the picture the handsome buildings of eighteenth- and nineteenth-century Teignmouth can be seen. Teignmouth was one of Devon's first resorts and the coming of the railway (to be seen running along the northern – right-hand – side of the estuary) enhanced this prosperity. The spit of land in the foreground provided a sheltered anchorage in the estuary, and the existence of a good deep-water anchorage off Shaldon (on the left of the picture) made this a centre of maritime activity. Today, after some vicissitudes, Teignmouth docks (bottom right) continue to flourish, particularly in the continuing export of ball-clay, and the import of timber and feedstuffs.

Shaldon Bridge was not built until 1827 – and it had to be rebuilt after collapsing in 1837. Before that the river could not be crossed by road lower down than Teign Bridge near Newton Abbot, where the Roman and mediaeval river crossings were. The present Shaldon Bridge, shown here, was built in 1927.

Further Reading

Trump, H. *West Country Harbour* (Brunswick Press 1976) (2nd ed. published in 1986 as *Teignmouth. A Maritime History*)

Photograph: J.K.S. St. Joseph, Cambridge University, 23 June 1952 (Crown copyright)

Plate 97

Newquay, on the River Tamar

Newquay lies on the Devon bank of the Tamar, about 1 km south of the better-known port of Morwellham. There was a small quay here in the woodland by the mid eighteenth century, but this was greatly expanded in the 1840s and 1850s to its present size, visible in this photograph. The reason for the increase in the need for quay space along the Tamar at that time, at Morwellham, Newquay and lower down the river at Gawton as well, was the enormous expansion in the mining industry of the surrounding area and the consequent need for shipping facilities to take the products down the river by boat. Devon Great Consols was the single biggest mine in the area, producing principally copper and arsenic, but the quays here served a large hinterland. As was the case at Bude (above), the coming of the railway in 1859 brought the shipping boom to an abrupt halt, and Newquay fell quickly into decay. We thus see the village of the 1850s virtually unaffected by later development in this picture.

The large quay area fronting the river was constructed in the mid nineteenth century; the two small docks on the opposite side of the river are probably a little earlier. On the waterfront are small yards for dividing up the cargoes of ores. In the wall at the back of the village (not visible here, but almost underneath the position of the camera) are a series of ore-chutes, down which the minerals for shipping were tipped from the road at the back of the site on to the quay.

In the centre of the picture there are the remains of the buildings associated with Newquay's inward trade, particularly the import of limestone and coal which were burnt for fertilizer. The wells of three limekilns are visible, while the steeply sloping wall-like structure running up from the river to their right is an inclined plane which carried a tramway; this enabled trucks loaded with the coal and limestone to be drawn from the level of the quay to the top of the kilns. The trucks were pulled up by a water-wheel in a pit which can just be glimpsed in the trees to the right of the inclined plane. The water-wheel was in turn driven by water from a leat just off the bottom of the picture. The remainder of the buildings in the photograph housed the permanent inhabitants of this once thriving community: there are a series of cottages, stables and, nearest the limekilns, an inn.

Further Reading

Booker, F. *Industrial Archaeology of the Tamar Valley* (David & Charles, 1967, rev. ed. 1971)

Gaskell Brown, C. 'The Archaeology of New Quay, Devon', *TDA* 114 (1982), 133–68

Photograph: F.M. Griffith, Devon County Council, 21 January 1988

Plates 98–100

Clayworkings

The abandoned remains of the Redlake China Clay Works are a good example of a medium-sized extractive works dating from around the turn of the century. 'China clay' is kaolin: a material formed by the decomposition of granite. Much of southern and south-western Dartmoor is covered by deposits of this sort. The first known reference to a china-clay pit *per se* is found in a document of 1502 and relates to a pit at Hook Lake, not far from Redlake. It was not until the earlier part of the nineteenth century that the Dartmoor deposits were extensively worked – rather later than the inception of the industry in Cornwall.

The earliest extractive efforts at Redlake were directed not at the china clay but at the surface peat deposits, which, particularly in the mid part of the nineteenth century, were being quarried in many parts of the moor in an attempt to produce commercially viable quantities of peat, peat charcoal and naphtha. The area around Redlake was briefly exploited in this way from 1846 to 1850, the peat being removed to Shipley Bridge by tramway for processing. This industry was, however, soon rendered uneconomic by the rapid growth of the use of town gas as a fuel.

The works now visible at Redlake are the result of a venture by the China Clay Corporation, a company formed for the purpose in 1910. Prospecting in the area had been carried out since 1905; the civil engineer employed on the project was R. Hansford Worth, better known to us as Dartmoor's most celebrated archaeologist. Production began in 1914, using a labour force many of whom lodged in a hostel on site all week. The tramway visible in the photograph was not for the removal of the clay (which was pumped through a pipeline down to the Great Western Railway at Cantrell, near Ivybridge) but for transport of the workforce and to keep the works supplied with fuel and other necessities. The picture also shows the claypit itself. The conical spoilheap is characteristic of clayworkings of this date: modern safety regulations require a much flatter stepped profile to waste heaps. The works at Redlake suffered a long period of decline and finally closed in 1932, when the machinery and rolling stock of the mine and tramway were dispersed.

China clay is still an important commodity, and its quarrying is a major industry in both Devon and Cornwall. As this picture of the Lee Moor works on south-west Dartmoor shows, the scale of the modern industry is very different from that of eighty years ago.

The Left Lake Clayworks was roughly contemporary with Redlake. The settling pits can clearly be seen.

Further Reading

Harris, H. *The Industrial Archaeology of Dartmoor* (David & Charles, 1968 rev. ed. 1987)

Wade, E. A. *The Redlake Tramway and China Clay Works* (Twelveheads Press, 1982)

Plate 98 Left Lake Clayworks *Photograph: F.M. Griffith, Devon County Council, 20 March 1987*

Plate 99 Redlake Clayworks *Photograph: F.M. Griffith, Devon*

l, 16 February 1988

Plate 100 Lee Moor Clayworks *Photograph: National Monuments Record, RCHME, 20 May 1977*

Plate 101

Nineteenth-century Churches, St Marychurch, Torquay

In the earlier part of the nineteenth century the previously small village of Torquay suddenly experienced a great boom as a resort, in particular for weak and consumptive people. This development was vigorously encouraged by most, though not all, of the major landowners in the area, who made large fortunes from the expansion of the town. Throughout the century, and particularly after the coming of the railway, the town grew steadily until it engulfed its northern neighbour St Marychurch, which in 1821 had had a population of only 800. This rapid expansion is reflected in the new building of this date seen in the photograph, with the two fine new churches (Anglican and Roman Catholic) that were built to provide for the spiritual needs of the prosperous new inhabitants.

The original foundation of the church at St Marychurch goes back to the Anglo-Saxon period, but the church on the site in the nineteenth century was rebuilt in 1856–61 on a much grander scale. The tower was built later, in 1872, as a memorial to the formidable Bishop Philpotts of Exeter who died in 1869. The architect of the church was J.W. Hugall, much in demand as a church architect at the time. This church (the further one in the picture) was damaged in the blitz and has since been extensively rebuilt. In the foreground can be seen the Catholic church, Our Lady Help of Christians, built in 1865, with its attached presbytery and orphanage, to a design by Hansom. The spire is unusually tall for a Devon church and the splendid tower of St Mary may have been built as a riposte to it.

Further Reading

Russell, P. *A History of Torquay and the Famous Anchorage of Torbay* (Torquay Natural History Society, 1960)

Photograph: F.M. Griffith, Devon County Council, 21 December 1986

Plate 102

Exe Vale Hospital, Exminster

The aerial view is an ideal way to appreciate the pioneering layout of this striking building: although it is visible, for example, from the M5 its layout cannot be understood from such an angle. It is interesting that, in order to illustrate a paper about the building written in 1845, the architect drew a bird's eye 'aerial perspective' of the hospital very similar to this photograph.

The hospital was built as the Devon County Lunatic Asylum in 1842–5: a response to the special requirements of 'pauper lunatics', i.e. those who could not be appropriately looked after in the normal workhouse under the Poor Law of 1834. The architect was the celebrated Charles Fowler, a Devon man from Cullompton who had already achieved recognition as the architect of Covent Garden Market, as well as the Higher and Lower Markets in Exeter. In this hospital he applied the same functional approach as he had to other public buildings, resulting in an exceptionally enlightened and radical design, which provided airy wards for the patients, a farm where they grew their own food, and a layout of wards radiating from a central service block which permitted the efficient use of staff and avoided the need to deliver meals from the kitchen by horse and cart, as was the case in some establishments of the time.

The future of Exe Vale Hospital is at the time of writing in some doubt. Under the proposals to offer care for patients 'in the community' the hospital is about to become surplus to NHS requirements. At present an alternative use for this impressive building (its importance now recognized by its listing as a Grade II* Building of Historic Interest) is being sought. One of the objectives of the current programme of aerial photography in Devon is to record buildings and other elements of the landscape which may be about to experience some change from their original appearance.

Further Reading

Brooks, C. and Cox, J. 'Charles Fowler and the Devon County Asylum, Exminster', *DBG Newsletter* 1 (April 1986), 11–14

Photograph: F.M. Griffith, Devon County Council, 6 March 1986

Plate 103

Buckfast Abbey

Buckfast Abbey was founded on the west bank of the River Dart in 1018. Originally a Benedictine house, it was subsequently granted to Savigny in 1136, and in 1147 its monks joined the Cistercian community. After the Dissolution the abbey buildings fell into decay, and in 1806 much of the site was levelled for the construction of the large woollen-mill complex seen in the foreground of this picture: the riverside location for power (the Dart can be seen top right) and the ready supply of building stone from the abbey ruins made it an ideal site for the mill.

The Buckfast Abbey we see here was built by a fraternity of Benedictine monks who came from France in 1882 to refound the monastery: the work was finally completed in 1932. The great church and cloister are built in Norman/Early Gothic style, but incorporate some earlier survivals. At the corner of the cloister nearest the camera a fifteenth-century tower can just be seen. The Abbey Gatehouse, seen crossing the road at the entrance to the site, is another mediaeval survival, and recent archaeological recording work has identified substantial remains of other mediaeval structures, including the Guest Hall, in the standing buildings to the west (left) of the road.

Since 1982, excavations by Stewart Brown on the site of the new car park and visitor centre to the left of the picture have uncovered the remains of some of the buildings of the monastery's Outer Court, where most of the day-to-day practical affairs of the mediaeval abbey took place. The results of these excavations, and of the associated building recording work, can be seen in an exhibition at the visitor centre.

Further Reading

Brown, S. 'Medieval Buckfast Abbey', *Devon Archaeol.* 1 (1983), 8–11

— 'Excavations and Building Recording in 1982 and 1984 at Buckfast Abbey', *PDAS* in press

Stephan, Dom. J. *A History of Buckfast Abbey from 1018–1968* (1970)

Photograph: F.M. Griffith, Devon County Council, 11 January 1988

Plate 104

Appledore Shipyards

Appledore is situated at the mouth of the River Torridge at the point where it meets the Taw. Its function has always been bound up with its maritime situation, and it continues as a fishing port to this day. It has also for long served as a centre for shipbuilding and repairing. In the mediaeval and early modern periods this would have been carried out on the foreshore as was usual at that time, but by the nineteenth century purpose-built shipyards were coming into use.

In the centre of the picture we see Richmond Dock, built in 1856 and said to have been the largest dry dock in all the Bristol Channel ports at that time. By the early nineteenth century much of the timber for shipbuilding in Britain was being imported from North America, the traditional supply from the Baltic ports having been interrupted by the Napoleonic Wars. Appledore was excellently sited to use the North American trade economically, but the business became more sophisticated when ships were rough-built on Prince Edward Island and sailed over to Appledore for finishing. Richmond Dock was constructed for this particular business, and prospered. Its especial importance in the history of north Devon shipbuilding has recently been recognized by its designation as a Grade II* Listed Building.

Richmond shipyard took its name from the North American focus of the Yeo family's trade – Richmond Bay on Prince Edward Island.

Photograph: G. Ward, Devon County Council, 9 July 1987

Plate 105

Castle Drogo

Castle Drogo is seen here from the south, looking across the steep gorge of the River Teign. The 'castle' – perhaps the last building in England to warrant the name – was built of granite from the Drewsteignton estate itself, in accordance with the romantic image of the man who commissioned the castle, the millionaire grocer Julius Drewe. Sir Edwin Lutyens' original plans for the castle were even larger and grander than the building as eventually constructed: the castle as we see it, completed in 1930, is only a quarter of the size of the grandest of his various schemes. The visitor to Castle Drogo can see the plans of Lutyens' other proposals on display, as well as photographs of full-scale timber mock-ups of other elements of the design – notably a great gatehouse – that were never built.

The handsome landscaped grounds visible at the castle cannot be seen from the house, as would befit a mediaeval dwelling. Neither has the castle any external drainpipes, as these too would be anachronistic. Rainwater – and just north of Dartmoor there is a lot – is carried from the roof in pipes concealed within the 1.8 m thick granite walls. This is one aspect of the design that has caused the Castle's present guardian, the National Trust, much trouble.

Castle Drogo is a unique site in Devon. One of Lutyens' most famous buildings, it is certainly one of the most spectacular and strikingly sited of all Devon's castles, ancient or modern.

Further Reading

Inskip, P. 'The Compromise of Castle Drogo', *Arch. Review* (Apr. 1979) 220–6

Castle Drogo (National Trust guide leaflet, 1975)

Lutyens: the work of the English architect Sir Edwin Lutyens (1869–1944) (Arts Council of Great Britain, c.1981)

Lutyens, M. *Edwin Lutyens* (John Murray, 1980)

Photograph: F.M. Griffith, Devon County Council, 9 September 1986

Plate 106

Floods in the Exe and Culm Valleys

Despite improved drainage, the valleys of the Exe and the Culm north of Exeter are still liable to flood in most winters. To some extent this serves to maintain the fertility of the good light soils here. Both air photography and archaeological fieldwork on the ground show that these valleys have been heavily exploited by man from the Mesolithic period onwards. (See, for example, the ring ditches at Nether Exe, plate 14, and the Roman fort at Tiverton which controls the top of the Exe Valley, plate 36.)

The aerial archaeologist can benefit from examining the ground under all sorts of conditions, including those of flooding. After heavy rain not only may damp marks (see page 9) or waterlogged features be seen on occasion, but in the right conditions a sheet of water in a flooded field may outline an earthwork only a few centimetres high with complete clarity as it stands just proud of the flood. In Somerset a previously unknown prehistoric enclosure was recently discovered in the floodplain near Ilchester by this means. The courses of old river channels, potentially preserving valuable palaeo-environmental deposits, can also be located in these conditions. The airborne archaeologist will therefore sometimes be found examining the countryside in conditions which at first sight might seem far from promising.

Photograph: F.M. Griffith, Devon County Council, 16 December 1986

Plate 107

Landslips between Axmouth and Lyme Regis

One of the newest parts of Devon's natural landscape is the area of the landslips between Axmouth and Lyme Regis. The unstable cliffs of the Lower Lias shales and limestones and the Rhaetic Beds are subject to frequent collapses and landslips, which have sometimes caused loss of life in the past. The most famous of all the landslips was that on Christmas Day 1839, when the configuration of a great length of the cliffs was altered for ever. As the photograph shows, the 'new' ground is readily colonized by vegetation, and much of this area is a nature reserve. The top left-hand corner of the picture shows a golf course. The Devon landscape continues to change rapidly in this area: since the beginning of the nineteenth century, for example, an electricity generating station, a sheepwash and a warren or rabbit farm enclosed by a large wall have all been established on the landslips in the vicinity of Pinhay.

Further Reading

Roberts, G. *An Account of, and Guide to, the Mighty Landslip of Dowlands and Bindon, in the Parish of Axmouth, near Lyme Regis, December 25th 1839* (1840)

Butler, R. (ed.) *A View from the Cliffs* (Devon Books, 1986), Chapter 2

Photograph: J.K.S. St Joseph, Cambridge University, 25 June 1955 (Crown copyright)

streets before the war. Above the Guildhall in the first photo is the large roofed area of the covered market, and above that the secondary school building (now part of Plymouth Polytechnic). Opposite, the Museum, built in 1907, and the Library can be recognized on both photographs, but the area known as 'Drake's Circus' is very different. In the modern photograph it is the large roundabout and surrounding area just below the Polytechnic complex; in the older photograph it is the tight circle of buildings almost exactly in the centre of the picture.

Much of the housing in the older picture dates from no earlier than the great expansion of Plymouth in the nineteenth century. In spite of strenuous efforts by the Board of Health to maintain high standards of building and public sanitation, the density of occupation, with its attendant health risks, is very noticeable. In the post-war photograph housing is confined to the periphery of the picture: the wide laid-out central streets, in 1988 pedestrian precincts, are predominantly occupied by shops and public buildings. The tall building in the left foreground is the Civic Centre; the round one to its left the new Theatre Royal.

Further Reading

Baker, O.A. *Plymouth, Old and New* (EP Publishing, 1976)

Gill, C. *Plymouth, a New History, 1603 to the Present Day* (David & Charles, 1979)

Maguire, D.J., Brayshay, W.M. and Chalkley, B.S. *Plymouth in Maps* (Plymouth Polytechnic, 1987)

Photograph: Plymouth City Council, circa 1938 (left)
Photograph: F.M. Griffith, Devon County Council, 16 February 1988 (right)

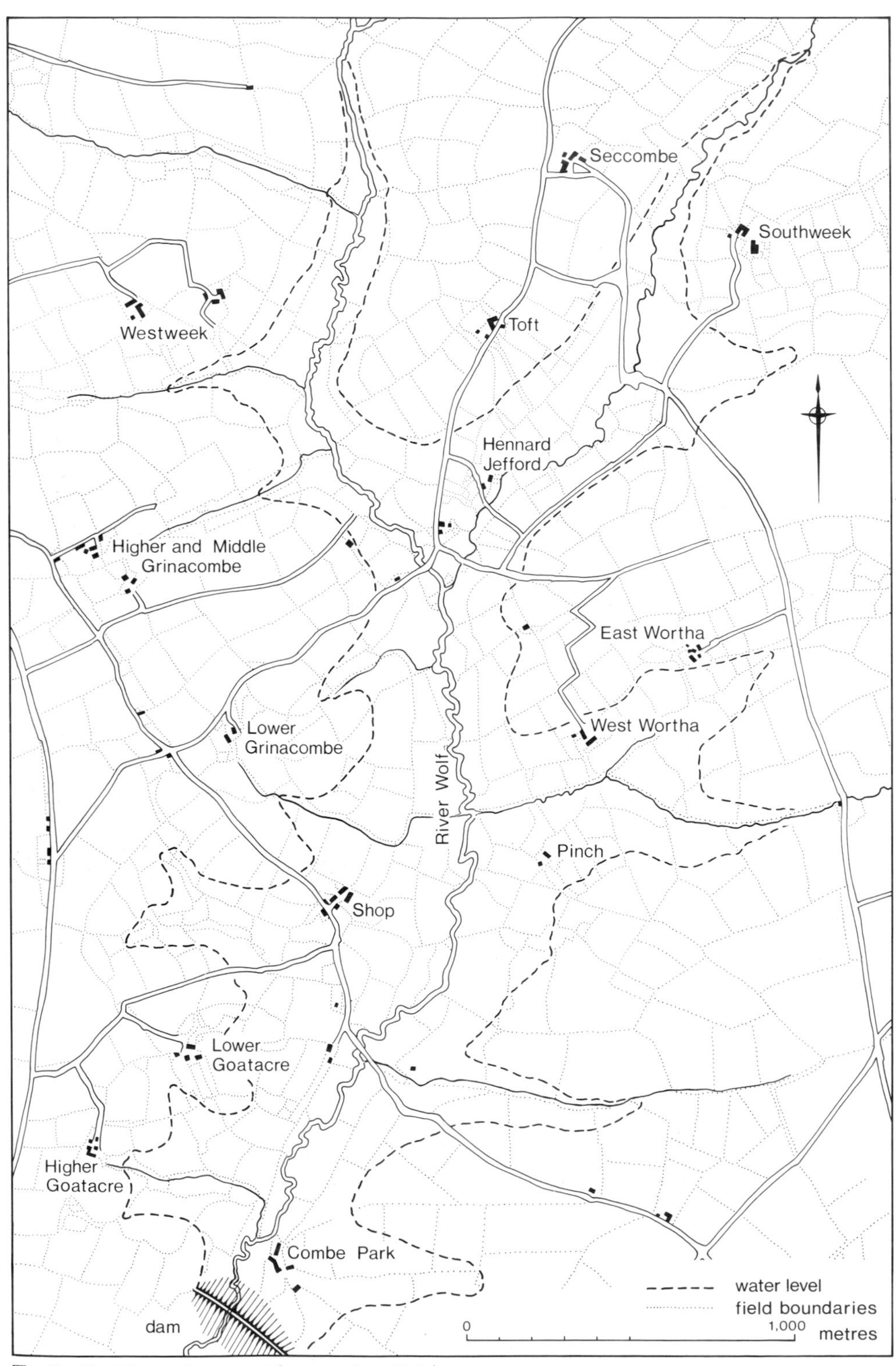

The Roadford Reservoir area: settlements circa 1840

Plates 111–114

The site of Roadford Reservoir, West Devon

Change in the landscape has been a recurrent theme in this book. Throughout Devon, from Dartmoor to the shoreline, the impact of human intervention has been frequent and sometimes dramatic. Changes in land use, resulting both from national trends in matters such as agriculture and from local factors such as the growth of Devon's population, continue to make their mark upon the face of the county.

At the time of writing, one major change taking place in west Devon is the construction by South West Water of an important new reservoir, part of their peninsula-wide water strategy, at Roadford on the River Wolf. The reservoir lies within a triangle formed by Okehampton, Holsworthy and Launceston. When full it will cover some 308 hectares and contain 33 640 million litres of water; filling is due to start in 1990. A large-scale archaeological project involving excavation, survey, documentary research and palaeoenvironmental investigations is currently in progress, carried out by Exeter Museums Archaeological Field Unit on behalf of South West Water, English Heritage, RCHME and Devon County Council, with additional funding from MSC through the Council for Christian Care.

The pattern of mediaeval settlement in the Devon countryside has been discussed above (pp 78, 90), and the point made that the hamlet, rather than the village, was the characteristic unit of mediaeval settlement in most parts of the county. Many former hamlets are known gradually to have shrunk to single farmsteads, but at most modern farms evidence of the former extent of the settlement is masked by recent expansion of the buildings of the farmstead, while archaeological investigation of its development is generally not practicable in the case of a functioning farm! The reservoir at Roadford, however, is situated in a part of Devon which has always been remote from the strongest pressures of change; in addition, the impending construction of the reservoir has tended to discourage farmers in the area affected from erecting new farm buildings for the last few years. The enforced abandonment of a number of farmsteads within the reservoir area, though a major disruption of the lives of the inhabitants, has therefore positive value in terms of historical research as well as of water supply, and offers an extremely unusual chance to undertake the archaeological investigation of the origins of permanent settlement in this part of Devon.

Plate 111 A general view of the landscape of the area. The high proportion of the area under grass and the large number of hedgerow trees are noteworthy.
Photograph: F.M. Griffith, Devon County Council, 14 August 1987

Plate 112 East Wortha Farm before its demolition. *Photograph: F.M. Griffith, Devon County Council, 19 July 1986*

Plate 113 Excavations in progress at the hamlet of Hennard Jefford. The standing house (bottom centre) was previously a mill, and the wheelpit can be seen to its right. Behind this building, excavations are uncovering the foundations of other houses of the hamlet: the remains of nine houses are visible.
Photograph: F.M. Griffith, Devon County Council, 14 June 1988

Large-scale excavation at several of the farmsteads within the reservoir area should provide information on the date of their foundation and on the way they have developed and changed through time, while it is hoped that fieldwork on a more extensive scale will clarify our understanding of changing land use and farming practices in this part of Devon. At present, more work has been undertaken on the origins of agricultural settlement on Dartmoor than in the Culm Measures that occupy so much of north and west Devon and north Cornwall, and it is really not known whether the farms and fields of these parts have their origins in the Saxon period, or later, or much earlier.

The Roadford project offers an exceptional opportunity for archaeologists to start to piece together the story of a part of Devon's history about which little is currently known. Like many of the other pieces of archaeological work described in the preceding pages, the investigations at Roadford take place within a 'rescue' framework but are at the same time the true stuff of archaeological research. It is through such work, and that of other long-term projects illustrated here, such as the Dartmoor Reaves Project, the work on the legionary fortress at Exeter, and the aerial reconnaissance programme itself, that progress will be made in the complex process of building up a fuller and more accurate picture of the history of Devon and its inhabitants back to the earliest times.

Further Reading

Timms, S.C. 'The Roadford Reservoir Archaeological Project', *Devon Historian* 36 (April 1988), 34–5

Plate 114 Combe Park Farm was one of the earliest brick buildings in the area – a status symbol in the early eighteenth century when it was built.
Photograph: Brian Lessware, South West Water, 1975